MW00880931

Clarity & Tranquility

Clarity & Tranquility

A Guide for Daoist Meditation

Translation and Commentary
by Stuart Alve Olson

Edited by Patrick D. Gross

Valley Spirit Arts
Phoenix, Arizona

Copyright © 2015 by Stuart Alve Olson.
All rights reserved. No part of this book may be reproduced or used in any form or by any means, electronic or mechanical, including photocopying, recording, or by any information storage and retrieval system, without prior written permission from Stuart Alve Olson and Valley Spirit Arts.

Library of Congress Control Number: 2015940934

ISBN-13: 978-1-5120-8796-3
ISBN-10: 1-5120-8796-3

Valley Spirit Arts, LLC
www.valleyspiritarts.com
contact@valleyspiritarts.com

Dedication

I dedicate this book to my wife, Lily, and my son, Lee Jin, both of whom have given me much needed lessons in life and a sense of joy that could not be in me otherwise.

Image of Lao Zi (老子) sitting in meditation
holding the pill of immortality.

Acknowledgements

I wish to deeply thank Melissa Middleton of Awakenings LLC for her generous support. Her investment and enthusiasm in this book is greatly appreciated and returned with deep gratitude.

To the members of the British Taoist Association, their financial support, friendship, and longtime encouragement for this work is nothing short of inspiring to me. I bow in deepest gratitude to their entire organization.

As always, deep gratitude to Patrick Gross, my longtime friend, student, editor, and whom I call "magic maker of books," for making this book a reality, and for appearing in some of the demonstration photos in section two.

Much appreciation to Lily Romaine Shank for all her support and encouragement of this book, and for appearing in the other instructional photos in section two.

Deep gratitude to all my students, past and present, for without their support, encouragement, and, even more so, their questions, I doubt this writing would have ever begun.

Contents

Daoist Meditation Method of Tranquil Sitting

Celestial Record

Introduction

Meditation (what Daoism calls Tranquil Sitting), the experience of abstract contemplative absorption of stillness and quietude, is not some extraneous condition to be added to your mental state of being. Experiencing stillness and quietude is an inherent state within everyone, a condition you naturally maintained in your mother's womb. But entering this mundane world with all its aggravations, anxieties, and perplexities gradually destroyed your innate sense of clarity and tranquility. Tranquil Sitting is a means of returning to the natural and inherent condition of your mind. Everything else is extraneous, not the other way around.

This book was not only written to help people rediscover their natural state of being through meditation, but it is a companion work to *Being Daoist: The Way of Drifting with the Current* and the forthcoming *Refining the Elixir* and *The Seen and Unseen*. Together these books will inspire anyone interested in meditation to become more diligent in their practice, and to bring greater clarity and tranquility to their life. The backdrop for this volume is *Being Daoist*. Much that is explained in that work reflects on the teachings presented here.

Although *Clarity and Tranquility* confines itself to the practice and philosophy of Tranquil Sitting meditation, *Refining the Elixir* will address the Daoist Internal Alchemy teachings, and *The Seen and Unseen* to the practice of Daoist contemplative meditation.

No matter the meditation method being practiced, however, people must first transform their perception of Daoism, especially concerning the philosophical applications of it. Meditation can

1

deeply influence and benefit our life, so we must first build a strong foundation on the principles of Daoism so that the benefits of a meditation practice can take root and produce positive effects.

Tranquil Sitting is a unique practice in that a person can watch someone meditating and really learn nothing about it. Meditators can't really explain what they experience when sitting in tranquility because they aren't consciously aware of it when it happens. I can no more explain the experience of meditation than I can describe the actual taste of water. Since antiquity, hundreds of books, if not thousands, have been written on the subject of meditation by people far more accomplished than I, but none of these works truly describe the experience. This is something you have to realize for yourself. The whole idea is to sit tranquilly in a state of abstract, absorbed contemplation, or as the main text of this work points out, "Sitting in tranquility even with no perception of tranquility." Meditation is a journey of self-reliance, self-determination, and self-attainment. No one can meditate for you. Only you can make the effort and experience the rewards.

The practice of Daoist Tranquil Sitting is not a religious endeavor, nor really even a philosophical one. It is simply a means for discovering one's Original Spirit, our innate source of being and True Nature of existence. Whether a person develops a spiritual perspective from meditating or not is unimportant, for all a Daoist cares about is entering the Dao, which is a way of saying returning to one's own Original Spirit or Mind, or as Master Liang liked to say, "To get out of your head and into your abdomen."

In my translation of Yang Sen's book on Li Qingyun, the 250-Year-Old Man,[1] there is a wonderful piece on tranquility, titled "A Discourse on the Movement and Tranquility of Mind" by Daoist master Haiqiongzi. A great deal of wisdom comes through Master Hai's words, and it lends much to the understanding of Tranquil Sitting and Daoist thought on clarity and tranquility.

A Discourse on the Movement and Tranquility of Mind
By Haiqiongzi [海瓊子]

When the human mind becomes active due to desires, it is like smoke pouring out of six windows of our body room, and wind roars around the seven orifices of our body.[2] The One-Inch Field[3] would feel thorns and brambles; the heart would be like a monkey jumping up and down. The dragon is sadly trapped in an ocean of desire. The tiger degenerates due to all sorts of affairs of the external world. The banks of life and death are spread widely apart. The distance between me and others is as high as a mountain. Even if someone's merit and virtue can fill up an entire forest, they can still turn into weeds. The family members that are now friendly may turn hostile to each other later. Even people who are

---

1   *The Immortal: True Accounts of the 250-Year-Old Man, Li Qingyun* (Valley Spirit Arts, 2014), pp. 336–337.

2   *Six windows* are the two eyes, two ears, and two nostrils. *Seven orifices* are the six windows along with the mouth.

3   *One-Inch Field* (寸田, Cun Tian), located between the eyes.

worried and distraught by a calamity, and then saved from it, could still end up dead in a cave of fame and fortune. The *Book of Changes* [易經, *Yi Jing*] says, "Fortune and misfortune, regret and repentance," all arise from these movements.

If people can keep the mind quiet when thinking, then the mind will shine like a sunny sky. The sea of human nature will be calm with minimum waves. The Elixir Field[4] will be energized like blooming flowers; the Hua Chi[5] will secrete a lot of water [saliva]. At that time, it will reach to the realm of forgetting outside objects and oneself, not caring about honor or shame per the secular standard. The wind in the pines and the moon in the water can become our brothers, apes and cranes can become our friends. Feeling happy in a silent sky, strolling on a clear and bright seaside. This is why the *Scripture on Dao and Virtue*[6] says, "All things return to their origin. It's called the stage of tranquility." And tranquility is the sign that that they have fulfilled their cultivation of Life [命,

———————————

4   *Elixir Field* (丹田, Dan Tian) refers to the area (or Qi center) located a few inches behind your navel, where the umbilical cord connects to the body. There are three Elixir Fields in the body—the Upper Dan Tian (between the eyes, or "Third Eye"), Middle Dan Tian (solar plexus), and Lower Dan Tian (behind the navel).

5   *Hua Chi* (華池, Pool of Flowers), the mouth.

6   *Scripture on Dao and Virtue* (道德經, *Dao De Jing*), usually spelled *Tao Te Ching*.

Ming].[7] I would grind up mouse teeth and sparrow's horn[8] in a place where I don't care. I would put a bug's arm and a fly's head[9] in a place where I don't go. If I have a Qin [琴] that can be played, I would play it during the evening moon. Would it be better than the Sheng and Yu[10] that gush through the ears? If I have wine that I can drink, I would drink until sunset. Would it be better than a feast filling people's eyes? Social hermits[11] can be friends to cultivate literary excellence with, and learned Daoists[12] can be friends with whom to cultivate spiritual excellence. Why should we envy that egrets and mandarin ducks can fly in formations, or can walk on the roofs of temples? Why should we envy people who can carve up a small

---

7   *Nature and Life* (性命, Xing Ming): These two terms are the main headings of all self-cultivation in Daoism. *Life* (Ming) is considered the "doing" practices, such as Nourishing-Life Arts, sexual alchemy, and so forth. *Nature* (Xing) is the state of "non-doing" and entering the Void, more succinctly the state of tranquility.

8   *Grinding up mouse teeth and sparrow's horn* implies litigation over trivial matters.

9   *A bug's arm* and *a fly's head* imply worthless and annoying things.

10   *Sheng* (笙) and *Yu* (竽) are ancient Chinese musical Instruments.

11   *Social hermit* (羣逸人, Qun Yi Ren) is a term for cultivators of the Dao who lived within society, reclusive but open to interactions with others.

12   *Learned Daoists* (羽人, Yu Ren), literally "winged men," meaning immortals.

bug and work very hard at carving a wood bug onto a table top?[13]

So, with these profound words of Master Hai quietly settling as a backdrop in our minds, let's begin the journey of attaining clarity and realizing tranquility, as there is a great deal to learn about the peripherals surrounding the practice of Tranquil Sitting. This is a worthwhile endeavor, and for those who truly apply themselves to this practice, the rewards are without limit.

Sections of the Book

This book is divided into three integral parts. The first part presents the text itself, *The Supreme Exalted One's Clarity and Tranquility of the Constant Scripture,* along with my brief explanatory notes on the fourteen sections that make up the text. Also included are definitions of important terminology used in Daoist philosophical and spiritual literature. This part serves more as the philosophical meaning of meditation, giving the reader the deeper reasons and conditions of meditation. The end of part one presents the text in English and Chinese (without commentary) for those who wish to recite the work for contemplation.

The second part presents an excerpted version of meditation master Yinshizi's writings on the method of Tranquil Sitting (靜坐, Jing Zuo). Serving as the physiological instructions for Daoist meditation practice, this section presents the somatic application of the philosophy given in the first part. Yinshizi wrote one of the best

---

13   Again, *carving up a small bug* and *carving a wood bug* imply having meaningless skills.

books on meditation because he based it on his own practice and experiences. The portion presented here includes the instructions he gives for achieving clarity and tranquility through the method of counting the breath to train both the spirit and breathing within meditation. This training leads to the more advanced Daoist meditation practice of Sitting and Forgetting (坐忘, Zuo Wang), which has some similarities with the Buddhist method of Chan (禪, Zen in Japanese) meditation.

The third part presents a Tang dynasty composition, simply titled the *Celestial Record*, which lists nine fundamentals a meditation practitioner should follow to truly attain clarity and realize tranquility. These nine fundamentals are more representative of the required psychology of a Daoist, as they act like a framework for how a Daoist approaches his or her cultivation practice for attaining the Dao. This succinct work outlines how a Daoist meditation practitioner should progress through the cultivation process.

The three parts of this book provide a comprehensive overview for anyone seriously seeking to master meditation. Although each division has its distinctions, they all relate to each other and must be viewed as a whole to ensure the meditation practitioner has not only the insight of purpose for Daoist meditation, but the correct method and a map of the plan for achieving the heights of meditation, namely entering the Dao.

Inner Meanings of the Text

The basis of the *Clarity and Tranquility Scripture* is to reveal the importance of attaining clarity and realizing tranquility through meditation, but it is not, as some writers have extolled, about eliminating all desires through moral injunctions or by conscious efforts to suppress sense desires. Rather, the elimination of sense-desire is accomplished by simply practicing stillness of body and mind, wherein sense desires simply cannot come forth. As the scripture states, "Tranquility without any perception of tranquility. How then can sense desires arise?"

Daoism is simple in its approach to the elimination of desires, allowing them to fade away of their own accord by following the influences of the "Naturally-Just-So."[14] As Lao Zi states, "The Dao models itself after the 'Naturally-Just-So,'" and so should the cultivator of the Dao. When a cultivator arrives at a state of clarity and tranquility, all that can result is the "Naturally-Just-So." No-mind, no-body, and no-conditioned things leave no ground from which a sense-desire can arise.

The Chinese term for "desire" in this scripture is *yu* (慾), a term specially used in the context of "sense desires." Both Daoist and Buddhist texts have adopted this term when speaking on sense desires. In the *Dao De Jing*, the term Lao Zi normally uses for desire is a different *yu* (欲), where the meaning applies more to the idea of longing and wishing for things motivated out of greed. In both cases, however, whether speaking about the

---

14 *Naturally-just-so* (自然, Zi Ran) is a Daoist term that refers to the spontaneous workings of nature and all phenomena. Zi Ran is that which is neither existence nor non-existence, or the reality of what is neither true nor false.

elimination of sense desires or desires of greed, the solution for their elimination rests in a mind that neither wants nor not-wants, as not-wanting can be as injurious as wanting itself.

In a state of clarity and tranquility, neither thoughts of desire nor non-desire can come forth. Therefore, the text states, "Continuously eliminate sense desires and the mind will naturally become tranquil. Clear up the mind and the Spirit will naturally have clarity. Then through the "Naturally-Just-So" the Six Sense Desires will not arise and the Three Poisons[15] will be extinguished.

The scripture uses three qualifiers for the term Dao:
* *Great Dao* (大道, Da Dao).
* *Constant Dao* (常道, Chang Dao).
* *True Dao* (眞道, Zhen Dao).

The *Great Dao* indicates the universal function of Dao, and is used to make a distinction between the universal function of Dao and that of a personal Dao. The *Constant Dao* is the eternal and infinite nature of the Great Dao. *True Dao* is the unchangeable and unwavering aspect of the Dao, inherent and intrinsic to absolutely everything. Regardless of the usage of the term, all three distinctions must be understood in the context of Dao as a

---

15   *Six Sense Desires* (六慾, Liu Yu) represent the sensual cravings and attachments to beautiful color, voice, smell, touch, movement, and features. The *Three Poisons* (三毒, San Du) of greed, anger, and delusion are considered poisons because when we succumb to any of them they act like toxins to our body and mind. When the Three Poisons are extinguished, then the Three Medicines of charity, compassion, and wisdom can come forth.

verb. In the Chinese language, Dao is not a noun, and it is the "unnameable" as Lao Zi describes it. In English, the term Dao would be better translated as Dao*ing,* as it is the active, everlasting, and unchanging function of absolutely everything, forever departing and returning. Likewise, as Lao Zi himself explained, the Dao is just an expedient term used to indicate something that cannot be named, and so the term *Dao,* alone, really has no true meaning.

History of the Text

The author of this scripture is anonymous and the text is believed to have been written in the ninth century during the first half of the Tang dynasty (618 to 907 CE). The text contains just three hundred ninety characters in ninety verses, and relies much on the philosophical ideas of Lao Zi's *Dao De Jing,* and in many ways rivals the *Heart Sutra* of Buddhism.

In the Daoist Canon (道藏, Dao Zang), the full title of the text is given as *The Venerable Sage, the Exalted One, Speaks on the Clarity and Tranquility of the Constant Profound Scripture* (太上老君說常清靜妙經, *Tai Shang Lao Jun Shuo Chang Qing Jing Miao Jing).*

It is usually referred to as just the *Clarity and Tranquility Scripture* or *Clarity and Tranquility of the Constant Scripture.* There exists both a short version of the text and a long version. The long version is thought to have been written much later, sometime in the Ming dynasty (1368–1644 CE), and is rarely used within Daoist studies. The short version is considered the original text and has since the time of the Tang dynasty maintained widespread popularity within the clerical and secular communities of Daoism.

The oldest commentary on this scripture was composed by the Tang dynasty editor Du Guangting.

Du claims the scripture was first put to writing by Ge Xuan, the great uncle of Ge Hong, the famous Daoist writer and cultivator in the Song dynasty who wrote *The Master Who Embraces the Uncarved Wood*. Because Ge Xuan wrote the following preface and postscript to the text, he has been said to be the original author of the scripture.

Du Guangting
(杜光庭, 850–933 CE).

Ge Xuan
(葛玄, 164–244 CE).

Ge Xuan's Preface

The True Person Zuo Xuan [左玄] said,

Those learned in the studies of Dao and who hold and recite this scripture will acquire the benevolent spirits of the Ten Heavens to protect their persons. Gradually, their spirits will be protected by a jade amulet and their bodies will undergo refinement by the golden elixir. The body and spirit will become wholly subtle and wonderful, and in true union with the Dao.

11

Ge Hong's *Master Who Embraces the Uncarved Wood* (抱朴子, *Bao Pu Zi*, Ge Hong's sobriquet) is the first written record of a Daoist's personal search for immortality.

Zuo Xuan, sometimes called Zuo Ci (左 慈), was Ge Xuan's teacher.

Ge Hong
(葛 洪, 283–343 CE).

Ge Xuan's Postscript

The Exalted One said,

> I say to you that the essences upon which you arrive at the Dao are limitlessly profound and mysterious. Reaching the Dao is to arrive at the ultimate point of obscurity and abstruseness. There is not even the nothingness of no-Dao.
>
> Guarding the spirit results in tranquility and caring for the body regulates the self. Be clear and be tranquil. Do not labor your body, do not disrupt your essence, and do not allow yourself to become either anxious or restless—this produces longevity.

The Jade Toad Immortal

During the Song dynasty (960–1279 CE), Bai Yuchan wrote the following comments on the *Clarity and Tranquility* scripture,

Bai Yuchan
白玉蟾, Jade Toad Bai
1194–1229 CE.

> The main theme of this text is to reveal that the attainment of clarity and tranquility are the source conditions for obtaining immortality.
>
> Therefore, if a cultivator's mind is able to experience the elimination of all impulses of sense desires, the mind will naturally become tranquil. By extension, when the mind becomes tranquil, the spirit will spontaneously experience clarity. Within clarity and tranquility, the Six Sense Desires cannot arise and the Three Poisons are eliminated, and the Seven Emotions[16] will be regulated. Through the inner vision of clarity and tranquility of the mind, the cultivator awakens to no-mind. Through outer vision of the physical body there is the realization of no-body. By observing these conditions as apart from the true self there is then the realization of the true condition of no-thing. When understanding these three [negations], only "voidness" is perceived as the true nature of reality. From this perception, all delusions and perplexities vanish, and so

---

16   *Seven Emotions* (七情, Qi Qing) refer to the feelings of happiness, sorrow, anger, anxiety, fear, grief, and love/lust.

the cultivator enters the state of Clarity and Tranquility of the Constant—which is none other than the attainment of immortality itself.

Li Qingyun, the 250-Year-Old Man While lecturing in Wanxian in 1927, Li Qingyun gave the following advice on Tranquil Sitting. Like many Daoist cultivators, he viewed Tranquil Sitting as one of the most necessary and fundamental practices for attaining longevity and immortality. Beyond Li's explanation presented here, see also "The Great Dao of Long Life" on pages 155–163 of *The Immortal.*

The Method of Tranquil Sitting

[靜坐之法, Jing Zuo Zhi Fa]

Meditation is the first important rule for the fundamentals of longevity. This stabilizes the Jing, concentrates the Shen, and controls the Qi. We had talked about its theories many times before, now we will only talk about the methods.

First, find a secluded spot to sit in, and construct a quiet room. The decoration in the room should be simple and clean. It should not have too much complicated furniture. The only necessary thing is to set up a Cloud Bed [雲床, monks' meditation bench], maybe a table with an incense burner, and a few chairs. No more than these.

The heart will be more easily cleared when surrounded by only a few simple objects.

The Putuan[17] on the Cloud Bed could be just a general sitting cushion. It should be soft and thick. Initially, when just starting to learn and practice, if the cushion is too hard, the feet may too easily experience pain, and this disturbs the Spirit. As time passes and a person gets used to it, then it can be positioned more evenly on the ground.

During the meditation, the clothes should be loose and comfortable, so the chest and the abdomen can expand. When in the Lotus sitting position [趺坐, Fu Zuo], place the left foot on top of the right thigh, then the right foot is crossed and placed on top the left thigh.

If in the beginning you cannot make the Full Lotus sitting posture, then you can start with the Half Lotus sitting position [半趺坐, Ban Fu Zuo]. The Half Lotus sitting position is to place the left foot on top of the right thigh and the right foot is underneath the left thigh. When feeling tired, the left and the right [legs] can be exchanged.

During the meditation, the head should be upright, the eyes should be half closed, the chest should be expanded, the spine should be straightened up, the two hands should be stacked or holding each other and the hands placed in front of the abdomen.

---

17 *Putuan* (蒲團), sitting cushion for meditation. Japanese *Zafu*.

The best time of the day for practicing the Lotus sitting posture is between midnight [11:00 p.m. to 1:00 a.m.] and noon [11:00 a.m. to 1:00 p.m.]. The first practices should not be too long, as the limbs will not yet be strong enough. If practicing too long, it may cause injury instead. You can use a stick of incense as a timer. Insert it in an incense burner. Initially, take the time of burning one half stick of incense as one session, then gradually increase the time. When one can sit for two hours, then there is no need to worry about sitting for too long causing injury. During meditation, the first thing to avoid is noise, the second thing to avoid is the mind wandering around. The third is to avoid practicing in a humid place. The fourth is to avoid letting the room get too stuffy and hot. The fifth is to avoid not being persistent. These are five problems we should avoid. If one maintains these problems, the mind and the Spirit will not be in control, and we should be paying more attention.[18]

Daoist Meditation Methods

In Daoism, two main streams of meditation practice exist. One is the subject of this book, Tranquil Sitting. The other is the practice of Internal Alchemy (內 丹, Nei Dan), which will be addressed in my forthcoming book, *Refining the Elixir.* Under the heading of Daoist Tranquil Sitting are two other methods, both of which rely on the fundamentals of Tranquil Sitting. The first is

---

18   See *The Immortal: True Accounts of the 250-Year-Old Man, Li Qingyun* (Valley Spirit Arts, 2014), pp. 201–202.

a method called Sitting and Forgetting (坐忘, Zuo Wang) and the other is called Internal Contemplation (內觀, Nei Guan).

For Internal Alchemy, four main methods are practiced, with the common denominator being the circulation of Qi through the two subtle meridians of the Du Mai and Ren Mai (up the back of the spine and down the front of the body), technically referred to as the Lesser Heavenly Circuit (also referred to as the Microcosmic Circulation or Orbit).

The four main methods are each associated with a particular text. The Refining the Elixir (練丹秘訣, Lian Dan Mi Jue) method comes from the work of the Song dynasty Daoist Priest Zhang Sanfeng (張三豐, 1247–1417 CE, also considered the creator of Taijiquan).

The second method is found in a work titled *The Supreme One's Platform on the Secret of the Golden Flower* (太乙金華宗旨, *Tai Yi Jin Hua Zong Zhi*), attributed to the Daoist immortal Lu Dongbin (呂洞賓, 796–? CE), but actually composed by Wang Chongyang (王重陽, 1113–1170 CE), founder of the Northern Complete Reality Sect (北全真派, Bei Quan Zhen Pai).

The third method comes from a work titled *Nature and Life Jade Tablet Decree* (性命主旨, *Xing Ming Gui Zhi,* appearing sometime around mid-1800s CE).

The fourth method comes from *The Yellow Court Scripture* (黃庭經, *Huang Ting Jing),* which is actually two books: the *External Illumination* (attributed to Lao Zi) and the *Internal Illumination* (attributed to Madame Wei Huacun, written sometime in second century CE). This method relies on the visualization of the internal spirits of the body.

The distinction between Tranquil Sitting and Internal Alchemy is that Tranquil Sitting relies on the practitioner attaining an utmost Yin[19] condition. Meaning, through gentle natural breathing generated from the Lower Elixir Field (Dan Tian) and an abstract state of contemplation, the mind experiences the Void, and through cessation of internal turbidity of the mind and external movement of the body, the practitioner will attain clarity of mind and realize tranquility of the body. From these three conditions of gentle breathing, abstract contemplation, and cessation of mental turbidity and bodily movements, the practitioner can enter the Dao and thus become immortal.

Those who practice Tranquil Sitting, including those who practice Chan (Zen) meditation as well, can experience the effects of Internal Alchemy just from their meditation practice, quite by accident, and in some cases like a side effect. Actually, the practice of all meditation methods are in essence Internal Alchemy because clarity and tranquility (or Chan/Zen) are about

---

19   *Yin* (陰) originally comes from the meaning of the "north" or "dark side of a hill," and later in Chinese philosophy was associated with the "female," "Earth," "dark," and "coldness." *Yang* (陽) originally comes from the meaning of the "south" or "sunlit side of a hill," and so is associated with the "male," "Heaven," "light," and "heat."

creating the conditions for replenishing the Three Treasures of Jing (Essence), Qi (Vitality), and Shen (Spirit).[20]

When I was living at the City of Ten Thousand Buddhas, numerous monks, nuns, and lay people related their experiences of feeling inner heat, movements of Qi, and fluid-like sensations within their bodies during meditation. These are all effects of Internal Alchemy. The difference is that Daoism pays particular attention to these effects and applies a mind-intention (or will, see note below) to their development.

In Internal Alchemy, the method relies on the practitioner attaining an utmost Yang condition. Meaning, through Embryonic Breathing the replenished internal primordial energies of Jing and Qi combine and are stimulated to rise up the spine into the brain, called *Reverting Jing to the Brain,* to congeal with

---

20   *Essence, Vitality,* and *Spirit* are the Three Treasures (三 寶, San Bao) of Daoist Nourishing-Life (養 生) regimes and Internal Alchemy (內 丹, Nei Dan) practices. *Jing* (精, essence) generally means the physical body of a human being. More specifically, the term is used in the context of bodily fluids—namely, saliva, blood, marrow, and sexual secretions. *Qi* (氣, vital-life) energy is the energy of the body that both heats and animates it, and is also the breath. In Daoism, two ideograms are used for Qi: 氣 and 炁. The first indicates a vaporous heat, and the second a formless heat. *Shen* (神, spirit) is what gives the human body its mental functions: mind (心, xin), consciousness and awareness (覺, Jue), and mind-intention, or will (意, yi).

the Spirit (Shen).[21] The process then of sending the *Elixir* (the combined Jing, Qi, and Shen) down the front of the body to the Lower Elixir Field (Dan Tian) is called *Yin Convergence* (陰 符, Yin Fu). Completing nine revolutions of this elixir through the Lesser Heavenly Circuit produces, in metaphorical terms, an immortal spiritual fetus in the lower abdomen, and from that accomplishment the practitioner enters the Dao and thus immortalizes his or her Original Spirit.

In some Internal Alchemy texts the basis for the metaphors used to describe the processes vary. Sometimes the analogies of a spiritual impregnation (the regeneration process), followed by a gestation period, and then a period of nourishing the spiritual child are used. Other works employ metallurgical terminology, borrowed from the ancient alchemy formulas of turning base metals into gold and/or forging a pill of immortality, using such terms as mercury, lead, forging, refining, smelting, and so on. Other texts rely on *Book of Changes* (易 經, *Yi Jing*, cosmological) terminology to explain the process. The majority of texts, however, use, in various degrees, the terminology of all three—regenerative, metallurgical, and cosmological.

Internal Alchemy does initially, and during certain phases of the alchemical process, use the principles of Tranquil Sitting, and it appears that with many masters of Internal Alchemy, they

---

21   *Embryonic Breathing* (胎 息, Tai Xi) is normally referred to as "reverse breathing." In "natural breathing," the abdomen is expanded when inhaling, and contracted when exhaling. Embryonic Breathing is the opposite. The abdomen contracts during inhalation and expands during exhalation, which is why it's sometimes called *Reverse Breathing.*

return to Tranquil Sitting in their later years. One such example is found with the great Internal Alchemist Zhang Boduan (張伯端, 983–1082 CE), who retired to a Chan Buddhist monastery in his elder years. This doesn't mean that his Internal Alchemy methods didn't work and that he switched to Chan Buddhism. There is really no difference, as sitting is just sitting. He didn't change methods as a question of religion or discerning one practice as better than the other, he simply wanted to sit undisturbed.

As Yinshizi stated, "Tranquil Sitting is the beginning practice, and eventually becomes the end practice as well."

Zhang Boduan, also known as Zhang Ziyang (張紫陽), is the attributed founder of the Southern Daoist Sect of Complete Reality (南宗全真, Nan Zong Quan Zhen). He composed two important Internal Alchemy texts: *Four Hundred Words on the Golden Elixir* and *Awakening to the True.*

Group Sitting Verses Private Sitting

Traditionally in Daoism there were no meditation halls or organized group sitting sessions. It wasn't until the creation of the Quan Zhen Sect (全真派, Perfect Realization Sect) that these venues for sitting were incorporated in the practices of the Daoist clergy. Clearly the use of meditation halls and group sitting were borrowed from the Chan Buddhists. In the Quan Zhen Sect, group sitting was called Zuo Bo (坐鉢), which translates as "sitting around the bowl."

Before the advent of Zuo Bo, Daoist cultivators normally practiced on their own. For example, in a Daoist hermitage, cultivators were left alone to sit in their rooms whenever they pleased. There were no scheduled meditation times, and really no requirement for sitting at all. Obviously, though, for people to leave their home, family, and livelihood to wander off into the mountains to cultivate, this meant they were searching for a place to sit in absolute peace and stillness, and reveals a very serious and dedicated frame of mind. As the Daoist immortal priest Zhang Sanfeng says in his poem *The Sleeping Immortal*, "How wonderful it is to be in the acquaintance of no one."

Living alone in a high remote mountain, how many of us could be at peace in the same situation as Zhang Sanfeng? Many years ago I lived in a cabin on a remote lake, and the majority of students who would come to visit me couldn't stay more than two nights because the quiet and solitude was too disturbing for them. Admittedly, the silence was, in comparison to city life, deafening. So much so that I found myself having to unplug the refrigerator and water heater at night because the electric motors in them would hum too loudly. Even the light bulbs buzzed noisily. It amused me to think that in the city I never noticed these sounds, nor the multitude of other noises generated by cars, street lights, and so on.

I mention that experience of the cabin because it is an example of what can happen in meditation as well. Normally we never hear our heartbeat, nor the workings of the breath in the lungs, and in deep states of meditation the blood flowing through our arteries. We don't hear these internal workings because they are drowned out by all the external sounds we attach ourselves to, and it is for this reason Daoist meditation practice incorporates the idea of "turning the hearing inwards," purposely putting all our attention in hearing these internal functions.

For some Daoists, a hermitage or monastery was too active for their likening, but for the most part it appears that hermitages consisted of just a few cultivators, more like a cloister. Some temples and monasteries housed larger groups of cultivators, but this was not the norm in earlier traditional Daoism.

In present times, group sitting is extremely helpful as it lends both moral support and discipline in sitting. Until a person is an avid meditator, it is initially difficult for most practicers to properly motivate themselves into sitting in a consistent and disciplined manner. Ideally, a practicer of Tranquil Sitting would meditate just as Daoist hermits did, alone, but this is not the best approach for those who are beginning to explore meditation practices.

Keep in mind that all the old Daoists we read about who sought to live deep in the mountains and forests were quite dedicated and disciplined in their practice. It is one thing to occasionally visit a meditation center or participate in a scheduled retreat, and quite another to give up everything to wander into the mountains to meditate full time. Modern society doesn't easily lend itself to this classical approach, so Daoist meditation groups are extremely helpful for people to develop their practice. Once meditators can sit with consistency, they are able to maintain a private practice and benefit from it. It does no good to be three days on and four days off.

Private sitting is the best, in my opinion, but only when your temperament allows for conditions to no longer turn you. This means, for example, that when you are getting ready to meditate and a friend calls to ask, "Do you want to go out for pizza?" If you say, "Yes," and tell yourself you will sit later, then you have let conditions turn you. If, however, you say, "I will be glad to go eat pizza after I'm done sitting," then you have turned conditions. When such examples no longer turn you from practicing, private sitting becomes very efficacious.

Using the Scripture

At White Cloud Monastery (白雲官, Bai Yun Guan) in Beijing (the headquarters for the Quan Zhen Sect), novice monks were required to recite the *Clarity and Tranquility Scripture* each morning, and it was also used for invocation and protection in certain rituals and ceremonies. Normally, a cantor read the scripture aloud while others simply sat in deep meditation listening. In other cases, the scripture would be memorized and recited repeatedly as a meditation.

In contemplation meditation, people listen to and contemplate a scripture, but not in the sense of attempting to understand the text. They just listen as though hearing the sounds of nature in the background. This is a very powerful meditation practice and, interestingly enough, allows one to absorb the teachings unconsciously when there is no rational analysis of what is being said. There's a big difference between understanding a teaching intellectually and experiencing it from a more intuitive state of mind.

Likewise, however, one should also study the text to learn the philosophy and subtle wisdom this scripture transmits. Providing a detailed commentary on the title and individual verses of this text would not only require a much longer book, but it's better for readers to gain such knowledge through their own consistent recitation of the work, which reveals its wisdom to those who contemplate and study it. The ideal is to memorize the scripture, then it is yours, so to speak, and the teachings contained in it will absorb into your consciousness.

This scripture is truly incredible, and if contemplated and studied deeply, it can change a person's perception and experience of meditation and life. It is little wonder why this short scripture was so widely and freely distributed in China, and why it has been maintained for centuries as a key and central Daoist text.

Achieving Clarity and Tranquility

Achieving clarity can be thought of as the mind being a glass of water with debris swirling around within it. The more the water is agitated, the greater the cloudiness becomes. False thinking is the debris, and the more we maintain false thoughts, the less clarity we experience. False thoughts are just the mind exercising its self-trained habit of conceptual thinking to keep validating the existence of the ego. False thoughts will keep coming until we learn to put them aside, and putting them aside is how we obtain clarity of mind.

Using the analogy of a glass of water, if we can just let the water sit without disturbance (in tranquility), the debris gradually sinks to the bottom and the water becomes clear. The water and glass are no longer murky and distorted, rendering a mind of tranquility that now envisions things with clarity.

Often people think that meditation practice should be about expanding the mind, having some type of ecstatic, euphoric, and mystical experience, or some profound flash of illumination. Although such experiences are possible, the more they are sought, the further away they become. The expectation for something to happen while meditating is merely the further working of the conceptual thinking processes of the mind.

True meditation is about not looking for anything to happen. The more you focus on a meditation method, the less extraneous thoughts will occur and the more debris you sweep away. Using a meditation method is like washing the mind of pesky and distracting thoughts, regardless of whether they make you feel intelligent or confused. The purpose of meditation is to bring you into a state of single-pointed mindfulness, and thus shrink the workings of the mind.

Two main problems occur when meditating to obtain clarity. One is confusion and the other is dullness. Confusion is a result of false thinking. It takes over when we become unaware of our false thoughts. As Li Qingyun puts it, "Don't be afraid of thinking. Be afraid of not being aware you are thinking." Staying aware of our false thoughts, then, helps greatly reduce them.

We experience dullness from being exhausted. This occurs from toiling the body, such as forcing a practice, fighting our confusion, or generally zoning out when sitting. In dullness, we either drift off into sleep or into a hazy state where we lose the awareness we are sitting. Zoning out does not bring clarity, nor is it a state of tranquility, or what Buddhists call samadhi (deep abstract contemplation) or entering sunyata (the Void). Dullness is the total absence of clarity, tranquility, and above all, mindfulness.

Confusion in meditation is cured by first being aware of all the false thinking going on inside the mind and then by gently telling yourself that you simply don't have time right now to think about those things. Tell yourself you will think about them later, not right now, and keep returning to your method. This way you aren't creating contention in your mind. Over time, the mind will stop producing false thoughts. This works because you are using the same method of how you train yourself to think false thoughts in the first place. We are the ones who give such great importance to certain thoughts in our life, dwelling on or even obsessing about them. When we do this, we push aside other issues and concerns in our life so we can give our undivided attention to the object of our desire.

So, by gently telling yourself you simply need to focus just on the method when sitting, the mental energy normally applied to false thinking will naturally and effortlessly fade away, and so without feeding the mind of this energy, false thoughts cannot exist. This is not a question of attempting to not think or to force away false thoughts, it is purely a matter of having awareness of your thinking and to focus your mind on those thoughts that pertain to your meditation method. Gradually the mind will lock into a state of one-pointed concentration where there is no more confusion or dullness.

Apart from abiding in false thoughts, the root cause of confusion during meditation is dissatisfaction, which, again, comes from wanting something from the practice. Maybe we want some mystical experience, or the sensation of Qi in our meridians. Maybe we want to fly or talk with immortals, or maybe simply just to feel calm. No matter what we seek, these are just wants and desires, and over time they make us become dissatisfied with meditation. Even if we are disciplined about our sitting, it can feel tedious because we aren't getting something from it. Meditation, or the cultivation of it, should not hold the perception of anything. Sitting is just sitting. Just like our breathing is just breathing, like our seeing is just seeing, and our hearing is just hearing. Do we really need to frustrate ourselves with all the distractive thoughts of what our ego wants from meditation? Just sit, breathe, and return to the silence within you.

Tranquil Sitting, in essence, is about returning to silence. Within each of us is a very profound silence, but our wants of attaining something from sitting only serve to interrupt that silence. Meditation sayings such as "returning the light," "turning the hearing inward," and "abiding by the Dan Tian" refer to rediscovering our innate sound and vision of silence. We experienced this when we were in our mother's womb. The Daoist belief is that we have no cognitive perception of external sights, sounds, smells, tastes, objects of touch, or concepts of the mind while in the womb. Since our organs and their functions are developing in this stage, a Daoist would say there's nothing to see, hear, smell, taste, touch, or rationalize.

The Six Sense Desires, Three Poisons, and Seven Emotions are not fully active and, therefore, there is no attachment to stimuli. A reaction to touch or sound might occur, but the conceptual process is not present. This won't occur until one is born and the umbilical cord is cut. The Six Sense Desires, Three Poisons, and Seven Emotions then gradually begin to develop along with the physical organs, functions of the organs, and consciousnesses of the organs.

The *Yin Convergence Scripture* (陰符經, *Yin Fu Jing),* which can also be translated as *The Scripture on the Seen and Unseen,* states, "The blind person hears well, and the deaf person sees well."

This quote is noting that when the physical organ and function of the organ are cut off (or not developed yet) only the consciousness and energy of the organ are present. Therefore, in the case of the blind hearing well, the energy normally used for the eye organ and function transfers to the other remaining sense organs, thus heightening the power of the other senses.

Lao Zi in the *Dao De Jing* says, "Even though the [sexual] organ may move, the infant has no understanding of its use."

Both these statements are describing aspects of the perfect states of clarity and tranquility. Clarity, in one regard, is the state of experiencing just the consciousnesses of the five senses. Even though their functions may be experienced, there is no attachment or conceptual process applied to them—which, then, implies a state of tranquility.

In Daoism, the meditation method of "Closing Off the Apertures" is about closing off the functions of the eyes, ears, nose, tongue, sensation of touch, and false thinking mind, and it is in this state that true clarity and tranquility are both attained and realized. Zhuang Zi describes this state as the person who when sitting in meditation appears like cold ashes and dried wood. Li Qingyun calls it "sitting like a tortoise."

All these examples come from the very early Daoist description of Hun Dun (混沌), the God of Chaos and Creation. The name literally translates as "muddled and chaotic." Lao Zi and Zhuang Zi use the character *hun* later in their works to describe the sage and infant as "nebulous and muddled." In Chinese cosmology, Hun Dun represents the "cosmic egg," wherein everything is contained and there's no aperture through which the contents can leak out.

These descriptions on the deeper meaning of clarity and tranquility are probably going too far for the purposes of this work, but what's important to understand is that the stage of being in our mother's womb is what Daoists would consider a perfect state of being. Because we are required by nature (our fate) to experience the trauma of leaving the womb, having our umbilical cord severed, and entering this external world, we lose our constant clarity and tranquility.

From then on, our immortality diminishes, but hopefully at some point in our lives, we undertake the work of restoring it. That is if we gain the insight and wisdom of seeking clarity and tranquility. This is what Daoist writings mean when they say, "Use the After Heaven to return to the Before Heaven."[22] All Daoist cultivators of meditation should keep in mind that obtaining the Dao is never about advancing to something. It is completely about returning to where you originally came from, a state of perfect sound and perception of silence, light, and tranquility. Lao Zi calls this the "Valley Spirit," our Original Mind.

Another matter for all meditators to understand is that Tranquil Sitting is not something you should force yourself to do. Sometimes we take on a practice and think falsely that more is better, or worse, thinking you *have to* sit. Both of these thoughts only bring confusion into our meditation states. It is far better to just sit when you can and when you feel like it. Don't try to force meditation into your life. Just as you cannot force desires out of your mind, you cannot force tranquility into your body nor clarity into your mind. The solution here is to let the sitting (and gently putting aside false thinking) gradually gain a foothold in your body and mind. This is a type of reverse process. Let the sitting itself cure the problems of attachment to the Six Sense

---

22   *Before Heaven* (先 天, Xian Tian) applies to aspects that are inherited, natural, and innate to our being. *After Heaven* (後 天, Hou Tian) refers to postnatal conditions that can be developed from our own practices, such as meditation. The objective of Internal Alchemy, for example, is to cultivate the "Acquired" (After Heaven) aspects of the Three Treasures to restore and join the conditions of the "Innate" (Before Heaven) aspects.

Desires. They will naturally fade if you acquire the patience of just sitting.

The *Jade Pivot Scripture*[23] advises us to use sincerity, silence, and gentleness. *Sincerity* means to trust the Dao within you, *silence* means to guard against attaching yourself to all the false thinking, and *gentleness* means to be patient with your mind and body during sitting, so not to create contention or toil within yourself.

None of what's been said here is complicated or beyond anyone. There really is only one problem with obtaining clarity and tranquility, and that is habitual false thinking. Ending false thinking always seems difficult to meditators, but really it is simple. Then again, keeping things simple is often the biggest problem for people. Everything in life, and in meditation, is just one correct thought away, but having that thought proves difficult because the debris from all our false and incorrect thinking obscures our clarity, upsets our tranquility, and weakens our immortality. Therefore, imagine returning to your core of silence when sitting. Perceive that silence you originally had when you occupied your mother's womb, except now it is within your own womb. When our umbilical cord is severed, a new womb, the Elixir Field (Dan Tian), is created within us. This is where our Original Spirit/Mind dwells. This may also be called our True Spirit/Mind, Before Heaven Spirit/Mind, Innate Spirit/Mind, Primordial Spirit/Mind—many names are given to it, but just know that is the place within your lower abdomen to which you return. It is where true silence and true light reside.

---

23   *The Heavenly Worthy's Jade Pivot Treasury Scripture*(天尊玉樞寶經, *Tian Zun Yu Shu Bao Jing*).

When our umbilical cord is cut, our Spirit/Mind conceals itself in our Dan Tian, and it remains there until we awaken it, or realize it, enter it, or illuminate it—all mean the same thing. It is purely a matter of using the After Heaven Qi to bring forth the Before Heaven Qi. So sit, breathe, smile, and return your mind to your Dan Tian. Stay out of your head and revert to your abdomen. As Lao Zi put it, "Empty the mind and fill the belly." Doing so brings clarity and tranquility, and from there we can attain and realize the Constant (Dao) within us.

Notice that I mentioned to smile when sitting. This doesn't mean making a broad expressive smile, but a subtle one. This is important because it will calm the mind and bring greater ease to your sitting. Smiling takes far fewer facial muscles, thirteen or so, than having a frown or some serious and intense look on the face, which takes seventy-four muscles. Just on the issue of facial muscle usage, smiling is far more economical. Smiling is childlike; frowning is like the face of a grumpy old person. Smiling can bring good health and energy to the body.

I've always found that when maintaining a slight smile during meditation, my sitting was more satisfying and far less arduous. The main reason for having this faint smile on the face has to do with the Daoist ideal of recalling our youthfulness, both physically and mentally, because as children we smiled frequently. I once read that a child laughs about three hundred times a day, whereas adults only two to four times a day. So, as adults, if we want more youthful energy, if we want to sit with greater ease and clarity, we can do so by employing a slight smile when we sit. After some time doing this, we may find it occurring more often in our daily activities as well. Even our dreaming may become happier and more at ease. Don't discount the value of smiling, as it is an expression of being serene and at perfect ease, the gateways to true tranquility.

To further understand Daoist Tranquil Sitting, two analogies are frequently used in various texts. One is the idea of sitting like a hen and the other sitting like a tortoise. The *Secret of the Golden Flower* comments on how the meditator should view sitting in meditation just as a hen does when brooding an egg. A hen sits upon the egg until the work is done, using her body heat (Qi) to aid in the process of hatching the egg. She doesn't worry, and is most likely unaware that it will take approximately twenty-one days for the egg to hatch. She simply sits and waits. It is a condition (fate) of her life, nothing more. Therefore, the hen does not experience dissatisfaction while sitting on the egg, because she is just doing her Dao of hen*ness,* being completely at one with brooding the egg. Meditators would do well to follow the hen's example, just focusing on their Dan Tian as though it were their egg to be hatched.

The other analogy is to sit like a tortoise, which can draw its legs, head, and tail into its shell and cut off all external influences. The tortoise can naturally return the light and draw the hearing inwards. Its shell becomes its womb from which nothing can draw it out until it decides to exit. No matter what occurs outside its shell, the tortoise undergoes no anxiety or fear. It simply withdraws into its own world. Meditators can learn much from the tortoise regarding their attachment and reactions to the Six Sense Desires, Three Poisons, and Seven Emotions—the root causes of all perplexities we experience in life.

With all the above said, the remainder of this book is about filling in the peripherals on the obtaining of clarity and tranquility through meditation. In truth, it would suffice to instruct people to just be clear in mind and sit in tranquility, because that is really all there is to meditation. Everything else should naturally just follow, but our minds will not allow us such simplicity. The mind needs persuading to change its patterns of confusion and dullness, for ridding itself of dissatisfaction, the Six Sense Desires, the Three Poisons, and the constant barrage of desires and emotions we invite into our daily life. To that end, I hope that the remaining portions of this book serve the purpose of helping us change our false perceptions and bring clarity and tranquility into our lives.

The Supreme Exalted One's Clarity and Tranquility of the Constant Scripture

太上常清靜經

The Supreme Exalted Venerable Sage spoke this *Clarity and Tranquility of the Constant Scripture.*

太上老君說常清靜經

Translator's Commentary

Tai Shang (太上), "Supreme Exalted," is an honorific and deified title for Lao Zi, the attributed author of the *Scripture on the Dao and Virtue (Dao De Jing)*.

Lao Jun (老君) is Lao Zi, but here using the term *Jun*, which means "venerable, sage, sovereign, gentleman, and ruler." When *Zi* (子) is used with Lao's name, this means the "philosopher" Lao.

The actual writer of this text is claiming that Lao Zi spoke this scripture, that these are his words. In part this is true because much of the text does come from the *Dao De Jing*, and the text on the whole reflects Lao Zi's philosophies on the *Naturally-Just-So* (自然, Zi Ran), *Active Non-Action* (為無為, Wei Wu Wei), and the *Way* (道, Dao).[24]

The term *Chang Qing Jing* (Clarity and Tranquility of the Constant) is referring to a state of long-lasting, eternal, or infinite clarity and tranquility of mind and body. The meaning of Chang (常) is taken from the first line of the *Dao De Jing*, "The Dao that can be Dao'ed is

---

24   See *Being Daoist: The Way of Drifting with the Current* for explanations on these and other Daoist philosophies.

not the infinite Dao,"[25] or as most translations phrase it, "The Dao that can be *spoken of* is not the Constant Dao."

So, the opening title here is explaining that the deified Lao Zi (Tai Shang Lao Jun) is explaining the meaning of clarity and tranquility in context with the infinite and everlasting Dao.

25　道可道非常道 (Dao Ke Dao Fei Chang Dao). The usage of "Dao'ed" in translating *Dao Ke Dao* is to emphasize the active principle of Dao being Dao, like saying, "the walk that can be walked." Most translations of *Dao Ke Dao,* however, use "spoken of" because they are only defining "Dao" as a noun. The Chinese ideogram for Dao (道), however, shows a person drifting with the current along a watercourse way, going with the flow or following the natural course of matters. This usage of Dao, then, is expressing Dao in the active sense, as a verb. Just as "walk" can be a noun and verb, so also can Dao.

2

The Venerable Sage said, "The Great Dao is without form, yet it gave birth to Heaven and Earth. The Great Dao is without impulse, yet it revolves and gives motion to the Sun and Moon. The Great Dao is without name, yet it eternally nourishes the Myriad Things. I do not know its name, but if pressed to give it a name, I would call it Dao."

老 君 曰 ， 大 道 無 形 ， 生 育 天 地 ． 大 道 無 情 ，
運 行 日 月 ． 大 道 無 名 ， 長 養 萬 物 ．
吾 不 知 其 名 ， 強 名 曰 道 ．

Translator's Commentary

The Great Dao encompasses the entire universe and all that is contained within it, but it is not bound by limits. Attempting to define the Great Dao can't be done, as it is everlasting and beyond defining characteristics. It is not Heaven (or the universe) nor is it Earth (Nature itself), yet everything is contained within it, being infinite and all-pervasive. As the text states, it gave birth to (created) Heaven and Earth, it gives motion to the Sun (Yang) and Moon (Yin), and it nourishes the Myriad Things.[26]

The Great Dao is formless. It cannot materially be seen nor can an image or personification be assigned to it. Talking about it only grasps at peripherals, thus it "cannot be spoken of." Trying to define it is like attempting to explain the taste of water. You can describe its characteristics, such as temperature, quantity, and color,

---

26   *Myriad Things* (萬 物, Wan Wu), the *Ten Thousand Things,* all phenomena.

but not the actual taste. That can only be experienced. This is true of so many things in life. Like emotions and events, only the experiencer of them truly knows what they experienced, and so it is with the Great Dao.

Note that the text says the "Great Dao gave birth to Heaven and Earth," not Heaven and Hell. Early Daoist works never mention the idea of a hell wherein transgressors are sent to undergo retribution for their misdeeds. This doesn't occur in Daoism until after Buddhism became established in Chinese culture and the gaining of imperial and aristocratic support became important. None of the early writings of Lao Zi, Lie Zi, Zhuang Zi, Yang Zhu, nor even the *Book of Changes*, mention a hell or hells.

Daoism believes people are punished for their transgressions, mainly through the loss of life span, experiencing misfortune, or making restitution through descendants (one of the reasons Chinese culture is so imbued with ancestor worship).

Hell to a Daoist is seen as an aspect of life here on Earth, wherein we fluctuate between experiences of fortune and misfortune. Since human beings are just a part of the Ten Thousand Things, the Great Dao brings nourishment to all life, but has no impulse concerning favoritism and retribution towards any living thing. Fortune and misfortune purely stem from an individual's will, intents, and spirit. As the first verse of *The Exalted One's Actions and Retribution Treatise* (太上感應偏, *Tai Shang Gan Ying Pian*) states, "There are no special gates through which misfortune and good fortune enter. We alone invite them in."

The Great Dao is not a god or gods, but they would be part of it as well. The Great Dao does not look down from on high and decide who should live or die, who should be rich or poor, or who should experience good fortune or suffer bad consequences.

The Great Dao is without impulse (having no desire or calculated plan), and it is nameless (appearing to be non-existent), yet it gives form and motion to everything in the universe and sustains all life and matter. However, because people have a body, are motivated by impulses, and need to discriminate the existence of things, Lao Zi reluctantly calls this unnameable force by the expedient term "Dao." Although he reluctantly gives Dao this name, the Dao itself is a constantly changing unconditioned operation of Nature, not a fixed and stagnant conditioned matter.

The Great Dao is our Great Mind, not the lesser mind that calculates, thinks false thoughts, and is distracted by confusion and dullness. This Great Mind is what realizes the Dao. It is what experiences the Naturally-Just-So, that which is neither existence nor non-existence, not real nor unreal, not true nor false. This is what Lao Zi calls "the mystery within a mystery," and is why it cannot be spoken of nor conceptualized or calculated. Later in the text when it states "tranquility without any perception of tranquility," it is pointing at this Naturally-Just-So, the Dao.

41

This section of the text could be interpreted from a cosmological perspective as well, and many writings on this work do so, but I believe this becomes too cerebral and requires of the reader a deep knowledge of the *Book of Changes* (易 經, *Yi Jing*) before a clear understanding of its purpose can be determined. In brief, however, Heaven and Earth can be presented as Qian (乾, ☰, *Creativity of Heaven*) and Kun (坤, ☷, *Receptivity of Earth*). Sun (Fire) and Moon (Water) then represent Li (離, ☲, *Distant Brightness*) and Kan (坎, ☵, *The Abyss*). Wan Wu (萬 物, Ten Thousand, or Myriad, Things) represents the 11,250 variations of the hexagrams.[27]

These four hexagram images then represent the process of Heaven, Earth, Fire, and Water as being the primary components for attaining immortality. This theory becomes even more involved when the influences and tenets of the Five Elements[28] are incorporated, as can be seen in the diagram on the following page.

There is nothing wrong with the cosmological interpretation, but it isn't necessary for the purposes of attaining and realizing clarity and tranquility. This approach simply provides another perspective on cultivation. The entire cosmological correlation becomes

---

27 See *Book of Sun and Moon (I Ching)*, volumes I and II (Valley Spirit Arts, 2014) for information on the *Book of Changes* and the theories and correlations of the Sixty-Four Hexagrams.

28 *The Five Elements* (五 行, Wu Xing) are the five elemental functions of Wood, Fire, Earth, Metal, and Water.

very complex; therefore, it can be more distracting and frustrating then helpful. In many ways, this is like thinking that one needs to know all the components and functions of an automobile engine before driving a car, which is incorrect. So it is with Tranquil Sitting, as the only necessary knowledge dwells in learning to "empty the mind and fill the belly," as Lao Zi so aptly advised.

Zhou Dunyi's Illustration on Tai Ji

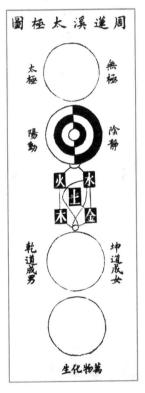

First Circle: Left side, *Tai Ji,* "Supreme Ultimate." Right side, *Wu Ji,* "The Illimitable."

    Second Circle: Left side, "Yang/Movement." Right side, "Yin/Tranquility." Left side of the circle is *Li* (Fire). Right side is *Kan* (Water).

    The Five Elements: Earth (Tu) in the middle. Upper left is *Hou* (Fire). Upper right is *Shui* (Water). Lower left is *Mu* (Wood). Lower right is *Jin* (Metal).

    Third Circle: Left side, "Completion of the male," *Qian Dao* (the Dao of the *Creativity of Heaven).* Right side, "Completion of the female, *Kun Dao* (the Dao of the *Receptivity of Earth).*

    Fourth circle: "Creation of the Myriad Things."

43

3

From the Dao there is both clarity and turbidity and there is movement and tranquility. Heaven moves and the Earth is tranquil. The masculine has clarity and the feminine, turbidity; the masculine moves and the feminine is tranquil. Originally these all descended from Dao, and so they flow on endlessly, giving birth to the Myriad Things.

夫 道 者 有 清 有 濁 , 有 動 有 靜 . 天 動 地 靜 ,
男 清 女 濁 , 男 動 女 靜 . 降 本 流 末 , 而 生 萬 物 .

Translator's Commentary

Lao Zi said, "Pure whiteness appears blemished." All things are thus marked by their opposites. No thing is complete unless it finds harmony and Oneness with its opposite. Lao Zi calls this "Embracing the One," which is a matter of following the Naturally-Just-So, and following the Naturally-Just-So is a matter of "keeping to being and holding onto non-being," as mentioned in chapter 1 of the *Dao De Jing*.

The existence of a self and non-existence of self, then, are just one thing, not two, and the "One" is Dao.

The text here is stating that the masculine (Heaven, Yang) represents clarity and that the feminine (Earth, Yin) is tranquility. The Jade Toad Immortal said, "The main theme of this text is to reveal that the attainment of clarity and tranquility are the source conditions for obtaining immortality."

To understand the Jade Toad Immortal's statement we first need to look at the dual connotations of the terms *Zhuo* (濁) and *Dong* (動). Zhuo translates as "turbid, murky, impure, and nebulous." Dong translates as "movement, to stir, to displace, and to alter and change." Next we need to look at Lao Zi's statement. "The one begets the two, the two begets the three," which is defining the natural or mortal progression of all phenomena and life, which is basically stating that from the Dao comes Yin and Yang. From Yin and Yang, the Myriad Things are created. In other words, the process of birth, life, and death of every mortal and living thing. However, in the process of attaining immortality, this progression is set into reverse motion. Meaning, from the three (which causes the Myriad Things), we reverse the process to enter the two (Yin and Yang), and from the two to the one (Dao). Again, this is what Daoist teachings mean by using the After Heaven (Life) to enter into the Before Heaven (Nature). The After Heaven is then clarity and turbidity, and tranquility and movement. Whereas the Before Heaven should be thought of as clarity and nebulous, and tranquility and transformation.

Now in the mortal progression, turbidity adversely affects clarity, and movement disturbs tranquility. However, in the immortal process, turbidity (the nebulous appearance) is the expression of clarity, and movement (the change and transformation) is the modus operandi of tranquility. So, depending on the progression, be it the one to the three (mortal) or the three to the one (immortal), the terms Zhuo and Dong carry different connotations.

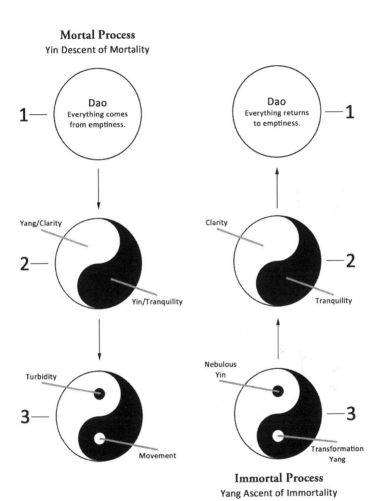

Mortal Process
Yin Descent of Mortality

1 —

Dao
Everything comes
from emptiness.

Yang/Clarity

2 —

Yin/Tranquility

Turbidity

3 —

Movement

Dao
Everything returns
to emptiness.

— 1

Clarity

— 2

Tranquility

Nebulous
Yin

— 3

Transformation
Yang

Immortal Process
Yang Ascent of Immortality

Later in the text it is implied that clarity is achieved by subduing false thinking, which agitates the spirit, and tranquility is achieved by subduing the perplexities that cause agitation to the body. Even though Heaven (Yang/masculine) is considered clear and bright, it is movement of the mind (the Yin/feminine) that disturbs clarity. Even though the Earth (Yin/feminine) is still and calm, it is turbidity of the mind (the Yang/masculine) that disrupts tranquility. When the mind is without movement and turbidity, clarity and tranquility can become One, the Dao.

This isn't so straightforward, however, because movement exists within tranquility, and turbidity within clarity. This dynamic can be seen in the Yin-Yang theory of the Tai Ji Symbol, the representational image of Daoism.

Movement (Yang) within Tranquility (Yin).

Turbidity (Yin) within Clarity (Yang).

In this symbol, the white area (Yang) contains a small black (Yin) circle, representing turbidity within clarity. The black (Yin) area contains a small white (Yang) circle, which symbolizes movement within tranquility. Within the interchange of Yin and Yang comes about the production of the Myriad Things (all phenomena). This is why the text states, "Originally these all [clarity and turbidity, tranquility and movement] descended from Dao."

How the Tai Ji Symbol and these Yin-Yang relationships between movement, tranquility, turbidity, and clarity relate to meditation can now be discussed. First, we must examine what is meant by "turbidity." Lao Zi uses this term in chapter 20 of the *Dao De Jing* to describe the mind of a sage, "My mind is like a fool's, appearing muddled and nebulous."

This statement is expressing the idea of clarity within turbidity, which can, for example, be seen in the countenance of an infant.

An infant's eyes (the expression of his or her spirit) are so clear and bright, yet an infant's expressions and reactions appear muddled and nebulous. Outwardly, sages, like infants, may seem turbid, but internally their spirits are clear.

Another way of looking at this is in the example of a hurricane. All around it are swirling (turbid) winds, yet within the eye of the hurricane is perfect calm (clearness). In meditation, we are like hurricanes. The world doesn't stop because we sit in tranquility or eliminate false thinking. Everything is still moving all around us, but we are like the eye of the hurricane, calm, still, and clear. In this regard, turbidity creates clarity, and clarity functions because of turbidity.

Clarity and turbidity, then, represent the external manifestations of the Dao, or as in the context of the *Seen and Unseen* (Yin Convergence), these are the *Seen* (what is visible and apparent, or as Lao Zi terms it, "being"). Tranquility and movement are the internal manifestations of the Dao, representing the *Unseen* (what is invisible and not apparent, or as Lao Zi terms it, "non-being").

To elucidate the concepts of clarity and turbidity, and tranquility and movement further, the terms turbidity and movement should not be taken in a negative context. Turbidity is actually the expression and basis for clarity. Movement is the expression and basis for tranquility. Clarity produces wisdom, which is as obscure as deep water, appearing muddled and unfathomable. This turbidity of wisdom, then, is the expression of clarity. Tranquility produces the One (the Dao). The Dao is constantly changing, yet unchanging. Change is enigmatic and implies something in motion, so the movement of Dao is the expression of tranquility.

Tranquility is what attracts the Shen (Spirit), and its movement is the mobilizing of the Qi (Vitality). This means that when sitting in meditation, the Spirit is to be retained internally (returning the light), so the Qi can be accumulated internally.

The Shen is what directs the Qi into the Lower Elixir Field, but can only do so from within a mind and body that have clarity and tranquility. In meditation this can simply mean, "Use the mind-intent (Spirit) to focus the breath (Qi) into the lower abdomen (Dan Tian)."

In meditation, the process is the same. When clarity and tranquility are attained and realized, the Essences (Jing) of the innate Spirit and Qi intermingle in the Lower Elixir Field. From this is produced the One.

Creating a mortal child is an After Heaven (postnatal) process, whereas producing the immortal child relies on the Before Heaven (prenatal) process. The achievement of clarity and tranquility, then, draws out and attracts the innate (or primordial) Spirit and Qi for the process of becoming immortal. Hence, when we practice meditation (Tranquil Sitting), we are using the After Heaven (physically sitting still and directing the breath to the lower abdomen) to awaken the Before Heaven (our Original Spirit within the lower Dan Tian). Again, this is all summed up by Lao Zi when he stated, "Empty the mind and fill the belly."

When we practice Tranquil Sitting, there's no visible evidence of what's going on internally, such as the movements of blood, Qi, and heat circulating within our body. Although we appear tranquil on the outside as we sit, a great deal of movement is occurring internally. Again, as the Tai Ji Symbol reveals, there is *movement within tranquility,* and there is *a nebulous appearance of clarity.*

My first true lesson in this occurred many years ago when visiting a zoo in Florida with my teacher, Master Liang. We had been walking around viewing the gardens and various animal life when I grew tired and decided to take a rest. Spotting a ledge with three crane statues on it, I thought this would be a good place to sit and rest my legs. I sat there for a couple of minutes, but when I moved to scratch my head, I felt the wing of a crane flap across the back of my head. My heart jumped to my throat as I ducked and fell to my knees on the ground.

I quickly realized those were not statues of cranes, but actual living cranes. When looking up, I saw all three cranes flying away, and could hear Master Liang chuckling. It amused him that I really thought they were statues. We then continued our walk and discussed the cranes and my delusion.

The cranes were perfectly internalized, with their breath and body so tranquil that no subtle movement could be detected. Master Liang described this as "perfect tranquility," yet within them all their functions of breath, blood, and Qi were moving. This made me think of Zhuang Zi's depiction of a sage sitting like dead wood and cold ashes.

Just as the Tai Ji Symbol reveals, *Embracing the One* means holding two opposites in harmony and seeing them as one. The commentary on this section, then, relates well to Lao Zi's statement, "Keep to being, yet hold onto non-being." By extension, one could also say, "Keep to clarity, yet hold onto turbidity," or "Keep to tranquility, yet hold onto movement." These statements are also variant meanings of "Keep to action (being), yet hold onto non-action (non-being)" and "Keep to non-action, yet hold onto action."

4

Clarity is the source of turbidity. Movement is the basis of tranquility. If people were able to constantly have clarity and tranquility, they would then understand that all of Heaven and Earth return to the Dao.

清 者 濁 之 源 ， 動 者 靜 之 基 ． 人 能 常 清 靜 ，
天 地 悉 皆 歸 ．

Translator's Commentary

Carrying on from the previous verses, the text is saying how opposing forces are equally the source of each other. Just as Yang is the source of Yin, and Yin is the basis of Yang. Day is the source of night, and night is the basis for the day. Male is the source of the female, and the female is the basis for the male. Black is the source of white, and white is the basis for black. Heaven is the source of Earth, and Earth is the basis for Heaven.

When we sit in meditation and seek clarity, this seeking can draw up confusion and dullness (turbidity). When we seek to be tranquil, this seeking can draw up agitation and dissatisfaction (movement). These desires for clarity and tranquility are just illusions of the mind. Even though we might want clarity and tranquility, the mind has no real familiarity with them. It does, however, have extensive familiarity with movement and turbidity because of the Three Poisons and Six Sense Desires.

Lao Zi advised, "Empty the mind and fill the belly." Emptying the mind brings clarity. Filling the belly brings tranquility. Heaven represents the head (Ni Wan),[29] and Earth represents the Lower Elixir Field (Dan Tian). Emptying the mind is clarity, and filling the belly with Qi is tranquility. When there is clarity and tranquility, one has returned to the Dao.

Imagine a glass of dirty water, with the debris swirling about (which represents the mind in turbidity). If we leave the glass of water alone, just let it sit, the debris will sink to the bottom and the water will become clear (this represents clarity). From this analogy, we can see that if we just sit and empty the mind, the mind will become clear—clarity will be attained.

Still water can be heated when the element of fire is put beneath it (this represents the breath in the lower abdomen). When water is heated it moves and creates steam or vapors (this represents the Qi). Steam rises, and in this case the steam (Qi) rises to the top of the head, and thus joins with the clarity. This then is the source cause for attaining immortality, the Returning to the Dao. It is so simple it protects itself from anyone knowing or discovering it by mere rational thought.

---

29   Muddy Pellet (泥丸, Ni Wan), top of the head. Also called, Cavity of One Hundred Returnings (百會穴, Bai Hui Xue).

— 5 —

Now, the spirits of human beings are fond of clarity, but their minds are disturbed. Their minds are fond of tranquility, but they are distracted by sense desires.

夫人神好清，而心擾之．人心好靜，而慾牽之．

Translator's Commentary

Returning to the Dao is easy. Just attain clarity and tranquility by emptying the mind and filling the belly, but for mortal beings this is very difficult because we are so easily disturbed and distracted.

We may all talk about wanting to have clarity and tranquility, as well as happiness, health, love, wealth, and to live forever, but we choose the wrong vehicle for attaining them. Somehow we think that if we are clever enough we will get these things. Somehow we believe that if we indulge our senses in pleasurable experiences we will achieve our goals.

Clarity, however, does not come from cleverness, and tranquility is not produced from pleasurable experiences. The vehicles of cleverness and pleasure cannot take us to the destination of clarity and tranquility. They only lead to disturbance and distraction.

Returning to the Dao is easy when we bring clarity to our Spirit, which can then see the way and not be disturbed or distracted.

6

Continuously eliminate sense desires and the mind will naturally become tranquil. Clear up the mind and the Spirit will naturally have clarity. Then through the "Naturally-Just-So" the Six Sense Desires will not arise and the Three Poisons will be extinguished. The reason people are unable to bring this about is that they have no clarity of mind and sense desires have not been eliminated.

常能遣其慾，而心自靜．澄其心，而神自清，
自然六慾不生，三毒消滅．所以不能者，
為心未澄，慾未遣也．

Translator's Commentary

The Six Sense Desires are the source for the Three Poisons of greed, hatred, and delusion. The Six Sense Desires represent our attachments to beautiful and sensual experiences. We desire beautiful and sensual appearances, sounds, smells, tastes, objects of touch, and thoughts. All these create the framework for our desires to continually seek out an easy life, a life of no bitterness and suffering. Some people might think this is a worthy goal. However, seeking beautiful and sensual experiences are what prevent us from experiencing clarity and tranquility.

The mind cannot be clear when it's filled with thoughts of desiring wonderful, easy things. Our bodies cannot be tranquil if we seek to only have pleasurable experiences.

All the sense desires eventually fade and become stained by dissatisfaction. The most beautiful appearance will become dull, the most beautiful sound will turn annoying, the most beautiful smell will grow foul, the most beautiful taste will seem tasteless, the most beautiful touch will be unwanted, and the most beautiful thoughts will cause agitation.

We can never really satisfy any of the Six Sense Desires. They are not constant, and have no end. They only breed an insatiable hunger for different and more extreme desires.

So when practicing meditation, cut off thoughts of good sitting and bad sitting. There really is nothing other than just sitting. Do not yearn for beautiful meditation experiences. Just sit and let the mind clear itself. Sit and let the body become calm. This then will bring you closer to the Naturally-Just-So.

7

When people achieve this elimination, they will, when inwardly contemplating the mind, see the mind as a false mind. When they outwardly contemplate their bodily form, they will see the bodily form as a false bodily form. So, too, when contemplating things apart from their self, they will see these as false things.

能 遣 之 者 , 內 觀 其 心 , 心 無 其 心 . 外 觀 其 形 ,
形 無 其 形 . 遠 觀 其 物 , 物 無 其 物 .

Translator's Commentary

Your mind, body, and everything outside of you are all false. They are false because they are not of the Constant. Although conditioned things are not infinite, they are in a state of continual change. A thought cannot last forever. Your body cannot last or remain the same forever. All things arise and then disintegrate. They are also false because everything—you, your body, and the Myriad Things—are nothing more than a perception of what we want and don't want them to be. All three falsehoods are not of the Constant because they are affected by space and time, the two main illusions of the mind.

If we do not have True Clarity and True Tranquility, then nothing we perceive is truly real. True Reality is not about what the false mind perceives. It is about what our Original Spirit awakens to, and that is Dao.

When sitting in meditation, it is always best to perceive all thoughts coming into the mind as just phantoms. They appear and disappear. All reactions in the body are just disturbances generated by the mind. All things outside yourself—sights, sounds, smells, tastes, objects of touch, or concepts of the mind—are nothing more than false perceptions,

When we truly turn our hearing inwards, when we return the light internally, and when we guard our Qi, then everything is contemplated internally. The Six Sense Desires cannot arise when we internally contemplate all things correctly.

To understand the three falsehoods of no-mind, no-body, and no-things, all a person need realize is that our past mind and body cannot be regained, both are gone and will never return. Our present mind and body change in an instant and can never be retained, and the future mind and body have yet to arrive and so we cannot grasp them. In other words, the mind is fleeting and like a phantom, but the Great Mind is both true and constant.

Many years ago during my stay at a Buddhist monastery I learned what these three falsehoods were really about. I hadn't really sat in meditation before going there, and neither did the monastery have any meditation classes (which struck me as odd).

Being a lay person, and with the rule that if I was going to be there then I had to do as the monks did, which meant waking up at 3:30 in the morning each day, undergoing a one-hour ceremony, and then partaking in two consecutive one-hour meditation sessions, with just a five-minute period of walking around the meditation hall in between the sitting times.

We sat on top of Chan benches, which were fashioned with a thin layer of foam cushion and a piece of vinyl stretched over it to secure it to the bench. These were anything but comfortable and being about two feet off the ground, beginners like me feared falling asleep and falling off (which some did).

For several weeks I struggled with sitting in meditation, and when I say struggling, I mean the pain. Every day I felt like my right knee was going to rip right out of my skin, my hips were in constant pain from sitting on the bench, and my back ached from trying to stay upright so as not to fall off the bench.

One day I could take it no longer and decided I needed help. I needed to know how to sit more comfortably. This had to be possible because I would see all the monks quietly sitting, motionless, and at perfect ease. Also, when a session was over the monks would simply get up and walk. In my case, I had to stay behind and massage my legs until they woke up and I could finally stand upright.

I managed to corner a monk in the kitchen area. He was kind of a gruff person who didn't talk much, but was an exceptional meditator. So I nervously mentioned my problems to him. He very kindly asked what I would do when sitting on the bench, so I told him how I crossed my legs, how I held my hands, and so on.

He looked at me, somewhat annoyed, yet managed a faint smile, and said, "That is correct."

"No, no," I responded quickly. "I can't be sitting right because everything hurts. My knee is killing me, my back, everything hurts when I sit." So he gave me some advice.

First, he said that my pain wasn't real. It was false. He told me that the next time I sit and feel pain in my knee, I should direct my mind to it and look closely for the source of the pain. So I took his advice and followed it the next day when I sat. Amazingly, after a few minutes of examining the pain, the pain moved to my ankle, so I examined my ankle in the same way and sure enough the pain went back to my knee. After a few days the pain gave up, or as the monk told me, the mind stopped creating it.

Within his advice, he also told me that the Chan benches in old China were called "Cloud Beds." The reason for this name was not so much because sitting in meditation is considered a lofty and high practice, but because if a meditator imagines he or she is sitting on a cloud, the body will become truly relaxed and comfortable. That little piece of information, when I applied it, totally cured my aching back and sore sit bones. In the end, all this taught me about my false mind, my false body, and about the false bench, because it wasn't a bench at all, it was a cloud.

8

When these three falsehoods are realized, only then is the Void perceived, but the Void must also be contemplated as being Void—a Void without there even being a Void. This is because when nothingness is Void, then this Voidness becomes no-nothingness. When nothingness becomes no-nothingness, there will be unfathomable depth, purity, and constant tranquility—tranquility without any perception of tranquility. How then can sense desires arise? For when sense desires do not arise, this is the Tranquility of the True.

三 者 旣 悟 ， 惟 見 於 空 ． 觀 空 亦 空 ， 空 無 所 空 ． 所 空 旣 無 ， 無 無 亦 無 ， 無 無 旣 無 ， 湛 然 常 寂 ， 寂 無 所 寂 ， 慾 豈 能 生 ， 慾 旣 不 生 ， 即 是 眞 靜 ．

Translator's Commentary

When we come to the realization of the three falsehoods —false mind, false body, and false things—we then begin experiencing the Great Dao. More accurately, we begin realizing our Great Mind. This cannot be described, only experienced, because to be in a state of tranquility where there is no conscious perception of being in tranquility is not something the rational thinking mind can comprehend. The problem is that if we are sitting in meditation and have the thought that we are experiencing tranquility, we are not really in tranquility because we are thinking about it.

Attempting to explain a Void where there's not even a Void perplexes the mind. Only the Great Mind can grasp this subject because the instant we begin having conceptual thoughts, we are retreating from the Dao.

9

The True and Constant respond to all things. Through the True and Constant, Nature can then be acquired, which is forever responsive and forever tranquil—Clarity and Tranquility of the Constant.

眞 常 應 物 ， 眞 常 得 性 ， 常 應 常 靜 ， 常 清 靜 矣 ．

Translator's Commentary

The *True* is a reference to the ideas of the Dao that precede the Myriad Things, and the *Constant* is referring to the infinite nature of Dao. Absolutely everything is nourished and influenced by the True and Constant. Concerning a person's meditation practice, the *True* represents their Before Heaven (primordial or innate) condition, and the *Constant* represents the actual immortal condition potential in each person. It is through the realization of the True and Constant that we then acquire Nature.

Nature (性, Xing) is referring to a Daoist term frequently used in these texts, *Xing Ming* (性命), which means "Nature and Life." *Life* is referring to the cultivation of Acquired Qi (After Heaven), and *Nature* to Inherited Qi (Before Heaven).

Acquired Qi can be lost if the cultivation is not maintained, whereas Inherited Qi, once one awakens to it, becomes True and Constant. In the *Jade Emperor's Mind Seal Scripture*[30]   it states, "One attainment is

---

30   See *The Jade Emperor's Mind Seal Classic: The Taoist Guide to Health, Longevity, and Immortality* (Inner Traditions, 2003).

eternal attainment." It is through cultivating the After Heaven that one can return to the Before Heaven, or, in other words, transform from mortality to immortality. So, Nature is really the immortal condition of all people, and it is through cultivating the After Heaven in fullness that the Before Heaven condition (immortality) can be restored.

Your Nature is actually your Original Spirit. It dwells behind your navel in the Lower Elixir Field, which is like a tiny womb in which your Original Spirit resides until death. It was with you while in your mother's womb, but remains dormant, in a manner of speaking, within your womb after the umbilical cord is severed. Daoist meditation practices, then, are about reawakening this Original Spirit.

Awakening the Original Spirit is accomplished through clarity and tranquility. Clarity allows us to see it, and tranquility allows it to arise unhindered.

10

Thus, by means of clarity and tranquility there is a gradual entrance to the True Dao, and having entered the True Dao is called "Attaining the Dao." Even though it is called Attaining the Dao, in truth there is nothing to obtain. It is only because of the transformation of a person that it is called Attaining the Dao. Those who have a realization of this may transmit it to others, for they are sages of the Dao.

如 此 清 靜 ， 漸 入 真 道 ， 旣 入 真 道 ， 名 為 得 道 ， 雖 名 得 道 ， 實 無 所 得 ， 為 化 眾 生 ， 名 為 得 道 ， 能 悟 之 者 ， 可 傳 聖 道 。

Translator's Commentary

From cultivating yourself through Tranquil Sitting, the mind becomes clearer and the body settles down. Your entire temperament begins to change, but this change is something you have had all along. Just as a caterpillar sheds its skin to discover a butterfly within, it was always a butterfly. It wasn't two separate creatures, but transforms from one appearance and reality to another. So it is with people, except that the Six Sense Desires and Three Poisons, along with a lack of cultivation, obstruct our transformation, our rediscovery of the Original Spirit.

However, as the text says, "By means of clarity and tranquility, there is a gradual entrance to the True Dao," so you need only to be patient with yourself, sit continually over time, and you will become transformed.

The Six Sense Desires and Three Poisons gradually diminish, your mind will become bright and clear, and your body will become light and free. You will also feel the Qi begin to move in the body and your spirit grow ever stronger and ever brighter and clear.

As you develop, you will realize that all these changes were already within you, and that all it took for them to occur was simply learning to be mindful of your Original Spirit.

And, when you realize your Original Spirit, it will seem as if what came before was no more than just a false dream.

11

The Supreme Exalted Venerable Sage said, "The high-minded person is without contention and the low-minded person is quarrelsome. The virtue of high-minded persons is that they do not seek to be virtuous, while low-minded persons grasp at virtue. Those who grasp are confused about both the Dao and virtue."

太上老君曰，上士無爭，下士好爭，上德不德，
下德執德，執著之者，不名道德．

Translator's Commentary

The high-minded person seeks the Dao, and the low-minded person laughs at and disregards the Dao. The high-minded person does not contend with others because contention only serves to create anger, hatred, or disgust concerning others and oneself.

Lao Zi said, "Because I do not contend with others, others cannot contend with me," but low-minded people quarrel with others. They quarrel because they seek to appear to be high-minded, but this is a pretense.

The low-minded cannot enter the Dao. They cannot attain clarity or realize tranquility. Low-minded people can sit on the Cloud Bed (meditation mat), but their minds are stormy, not free and gentle like a soft, billowy cumulus cloud.

Virtue in Daoism means having spiritual power, a spirit strong enough to induce good actions in others. It is not just about having moral correctness. High-minded people do not seek to exhibit their virtue, their spiritual power. While low-minded persons seek, through pretense and false actions, to appear that they have virtue, and through envy, to make others believe they are high-minded. This only creates confusion in themselves, and so they cannot enter the Dao nor can they acquire any spiritual power (virtue).

When sitting in meditation, disregard thoughts of contention, because once in the mind such thoughts will eventually express themselves in the body and depart from the mouth. When sitting in meditation, do not seek attaining spiritual power, because once in the mind this desire will eventually and erroneously express itself in false words and actions, creating nothing more than suffering and defilement.

Sitting in meditation must be free of inciting thoughts of contention and the pretense of spiritual power (virtue). When you find this freedom in meditation, it will naturally transpose into your daily activities as well, and then you will be one step closer to the True Dao.

Concerning meditation practice, it is crucial to understand that contention is not just about responses made between yourself and others, but more about contention with the self. Meaning, we can have internal arguments with ourselves about practice. Battling thoughts such as, "I can't sit today because there's too much going on," or "I'm too stressed out to sit," or "I don't have the energy to sit today, so I will sit tomorrow." We justify and make excuses continually about not sitting. Better to be like the hen, who just sits on her egg because it is her nature.

Sitting can become your nature if you stop contending with yourself. How easy it is to lay on a sofa and let two hours go by watching television. How easy it is to sit with a cup of coffee and just daydream for an hour. So many things we do have no real benefit to us. This is why I usually tell others if they could just get in the habit of sitting twice a day, fifteen minutes each time, they would soon find that sitting for thirty minutes, forty minutes, or one hour becomes easy.

But most people don't do this. They find reasons not to sit even once a day. This is an inner contention about not being comfortable within themselves. I once had a student who said he didn't like sitting because he felt he would be missing out on something else in his life, so he fought with himself about sitting.

All I can say, and I truly believe this, is that sitting is the most beneficial thing you can do for yourself. When you sit, you are giving yourself a chance to realize your true self. Nothing else you do in life does that.

Sitting cures so many ills within our mind and brings good health to our bodies. When you were in your mother's womb, you were sitting in perfect clarity and tranquility. After you left, your clear and tranquil state of being was quickly disrupted, eventually getting to the point of no longer knowing what it felt like.

We all think we know what it means to have clarity and tranquility, but if you are not sitting, being mindful of your breath, and reverting your mind-intent to your Elixir Field, then you don't really know, and you never will. This is, as an old Daoist verse states, "Living blind and dying drunk."

None of what I am saying here is meant to imply that we should be fanatical about meditating. I'm merely commenting about how much time we can waste in a day doing nothing of benefit to our spirit.

When you think about it, how many fifteen-minute periods in a day do you devote to being unmindful? The world, your environment, for those around you and for yourself, sitting only makes things better. A little peace is better than no peace, so just consider taking a little time each day to meditate. Be content in the gradual process of inching your way to clarity and tranquility.

12

The reason mortal beings do not attain the True Dao is because they have false thoughts. When there are false thoughts, the Spirit is agitated. When the Spirit is agitated, the Myriad Things are attracted.

眾 生 所 以 不 得 真 道 者 ， 為 有 忘 心 ， 旣 有 忘 心 ，
即 驚 其 神 ， 旣 驚 其 神 ， 即 著 萬 物 .

Translator's Commentary

False thoughts are those thoughts we engage in without any awareness they are false. We just let them flow unhindered as though they were the ruler of our mind, but false thoughts only usurp the clarity and tranquility of our true ruler, the Original Spirit.

False thoughts agitate the spirit. Like a thousand citizens constantly screaming at their leader, there's so much noise, the wisdom of the ruler cannot be heard. This aggravation from false thoughts causes us to feel our only refuge is in the Myriad Things—the world and all its affairs.

When we seek shelter in the outside world, our options for survival often take the forms of contention, interference, aggression, and conformity. We become like busy ants, scurrying about to survive and attempting to control our world. Within this turmoil, the spirit cannot function, it cannot shine, and it cannot be at peace.

In meditation, we must always be aware of when false thinking arises. Otherwise, these thoughts carry us unaware and unprepared to see the Myriad Things for what they are, the false objects of life that further confuse and distract our spirit.

13

When attracted by the Myriad Things, greed comes forth and there are then perplexities. These perplexities result in confused thinking, which causes further grief and bitterness to the body and mind. False thinking is then the cause for meeting with turbidity and defilement, drifting about birth and death, constantly sinking into a bitter sea and forever losing the True Dao.

既著萬物，即生貪求，既生貪求，即是煩惱，
煩惱妄想，憂苦身心，便遭濁辱，流浪生死，
常沈苦海，永失真道.

Translator's Commentary

When we are attached to things of the world, greed isn't the only poison that comes forth. Anger and delusion won't be far behind. The text is just being expedient here in referring to the Three Poisons. Whenever greed, anger, or delusion comes forth, we become perplexed. Being perplexed means that one or more of the Seven Emotions has become extreme and this is what causes us to meet with turbidity and defilement.

The Seven Emotions (七情, Qi Qing) refer to the feelings of happiness, sorrow, anger, anxiety, fear, grief, and love/lust. Whenever one of these emotions becomes extreme we not only lose the Dao, we equally harm our body. For example, extreme happiness injures the waist. Extreme anger damages the liver. Extreme sorrow injures the lungs. Extreme joy harms the spleen. Extreme affection damages the marrow. Too much fear will injure the kidneys. Too much love and lust will injure the Essence (Jing).

When these emotions become extreme, our minds are confused, and from this perplexity we can commit defiling acts. This is like being violently tossed about in a torrential sea where there is no contentment or ease, and no conditions for being within the True Dao.

— 14 —

The realization of the True and Constant Dao is a matter of self-attainment. Attain and realize the Dao of "Clarity and Tranquility of the Constant!"

End of *The Clarity and Tranquility of the Constant Scripture.*

真 常 之 道 ， 悟 者 自 得 ， 得 悟 道 者 ， 常 清 靜 矣 ．

Translator's Commentary

No one can give you the realization of the Dao. You must cultivate this yourself. By achieving clarity, the True Dao can be attained. Through entering tranquility, the Constant Dao can be realized. Although you must do the work yourself, the following nine fundamentals can help you achieve clarity and realize tranquility:

1) Correcting the Mind.
2) Curbing Sense Desires.
3) Sincerity of Mind-Intent.
4) Settling Anxiety.
5) Fostering the Essence.
6) Nourishing the Qi.
7) Concentrating the Spirit.
8) Contemplating the Void.
9) Become the True.

These nine steps, explained in the *Celestial Record* section, are most expediently accomplished through sitting, by emptying the mind and filling the belly, as Lao Zi instructed.

When sitting, all nine fundamentals are being addressed simultaneously. This is because in meditation we should enter a state of no perception of these nine fundamentals. When there is no perception of them, then they are complete. This state of no perception (clarity and tranquility) is how we can attain and realize the Dao.

The entire process is so easy when we can empty the mind and completely focus on our breathing (filling the belly). On the other hand, sitting can be very difficult if we allow our minds to be distracted by false thoughts and do not focus on the meditation method.

It all comes down to this point of either allowing distractions to fill our mind or emptying the mind of distractions. However, we must equally understand that having thoughts is not the problem. Being unaware of them is what brings confusion and dullness, agitation and perplexities, and greed and suffering.

When you are aware of your thoughts, you can regulate and deal with them so they do not become a source of distraction. When thoughts are regulated, there is then clarity of the mind. With clarity, the body can then be tranquil. This is all that need be said.

English Text for Recitation

The Supreme Exalted One's
Clarity and Tranquility of the Constant Scripture

[1]

The Supreme Exalted Venerable Sage spoke this *Clarity and Tranquility of the Constant Scripture.*

[2]

The Venerable Sage said, "The Great Dao is without form, yet it gave birth to Heaven and Earth. The Great Dao is without impulse, yet it revolves and gives motion to the Sun and Moon. The Great Dao is without name, yet it eternally nourishes the Myriad Things. I do not know its name, but if pressed to give it a name, I would call it Dao."

[3]

From the Dao there is both clarity and turbidity and there is movement and tranquility. Heaven moves and the Earth is tranquil. The masculine has clarity and the feminine, turbidity; the masculine moves and the feminine is tranquil. Originally these all descended from Dao, and so they flow on endlessly, giving birth to the Myriad Things.

[4]

Clarity is the source of turbidity. Movement is the basis of tranquility. If people were able to constantly have clarity and tranquility, they would then understand that all of Heaven and Earth return to the Dao.

[5]
Now, the spirits of human beings are fond of clarity, but their minds are disturbed. Their minds are fond of tranquility, but they are distracted by sense desires.

[6]
Continuously eliminate sense desires and the mind will naturally become tranquil. Clear up the mind and the Spirit will naturally have clarity. Then through the "Naturally-Just-So" the Six Sense Desires will not arise and the Three Poisons will be extinguished. The reason people are unable to bring this about is that they have no clarity of mind and sense desires have not been eliminated.

[7]
When people achieve this elimination, they will, when inwardly contemplating the mind, see the mind as a false mind. When they outwardly contemplate their bodily form, they will see the bodily form as a false bodily form. So, too, when contemplating things apart from their self, they will see these as false things.

[8]
When these three falsehoods are realized, only then is the Void perceived, but the Void must also be contemplated as being Void—a Void without there even being a Void. This is because when nothingness is Void, then this Voidness

becomes no-nothingness. When nothingness becomes no-nothingness, there will be unfathomable depth, purity, and constant tranquility—tranquility without any perception of tranquility. How then can sense desires arise? For when sense desires do not arise, this is the Tranquility of the True.

[9]
The True and Constant respond to all things. Through the True and Constant, Nature can then be acquired, which is forever responsive and forever tranquil—Clarity and Tranquility of the Constant.

[10]
Thus, by means of clarity and tranquility there is a gradual entrance to the True Dao, and having entered the True Dao is called "Attaining the Dao." Even though it is called Attaining the Dao, in truth there is nothing to obtain. It is only because of the transformation of a person that it is called Attaining the Dao. Those who have a realization of this may transmit it to others, for they are sages of the Dao.

[11]
The Supreme Exalted Venerable Sage said, "The high-minded person is without contention and the low-minded person is quarrelsome. The virtue of high-minded persons is that they do not seek to be virtuous, while low-minded persons grasp at virtue. Those who grasp are confused about both the Dao and virtue."

[12]

The reason mortal beings do not attain the True Dao is because they have false thoughts. When there are false thoughts, the Spirit is agitated. When the Spirit is agitated, the Myriad Things are attracted.

[13]

When attracted by the Myriad Things, greed comes forth and there are then perplexities. These perplexities result in confused thinking, which causes further grief and bitterness to the body and mind. False thinking is then the cause for meeting with turbidity and defilement, drifting about birth and death, constantly sinking into a bitter sea and forever losing the True Dao.

[14]

The realization of the True and Constant Dao is a matter of self-attainment. Attain and realize the Dao of "Clarity and Tranquility of the Constant!"

End of *The Clarity and Tranquility of the Constant Scripture.*

Chinese Text and Pinyin
for Recitation

太上常清靜經
Tài Shàng Cháng Qīng Jìng Jīng

[1]

太上老君說常清靜經
Tài Shàng Lǎo Jūn Shuō Cháng Qīng Jìng Jīng

[2]

老君曰，大道無形，生育天地．大道無情，
運行日月．
Lǎo jūn yuē, dà dào wú xíng, shēng yù tiān de. Dà dào wú qíng,
yùn xíng rì yuè.

大道無名，長養萬物．吾不知其名，
強名曰道．
Dà dào wú míng, zhǎng yǎng wàn wù. Wú bù zhī qí míng,
qiáng míng yuē dào.

[3]

夫道者有清有濁，有動有靜．天動地靜，
男清女濁．
Fū dào zhě yǒu qīng yǒu zhuó, yǒu dòng yǒu jìng. Tiān dòng
de jìng, nán qīng nǚ zhuó.

男動女靜．降本流末，而生萬物．
Nán dòng nǚ jìng. Jiàng běn liú mò, ér shēng wàn wù.

[4]

清者濁之源，動者靜之基．人能常清靜，
天地悉皆歸．

Qīng zhě zhuó zhī yuán, dòng zhě jìng zhī jī. Rén néng cháng qīng jìng, tiān de xī jiē guī.

[5]

夫人神好清，而心擾之．人心好靜，
而慾牽之．

Fū rén shén hǎo qīng, ér xīn rǎo zhī. Rén xīn hǎo jìng, ér yù qiān zhī.

[6]

常能遣其慾，而心自靜．澄其心，而神自清，
Cháng néng qiǎn qí yù, ér xīn zì jìng. Chéng qí xīn, ér shén zì qīng,

自然六慾不生，三毒消滅．所以不能者，
為心未澄，
Zì rán liù yù bù shēng, sān dú xiāo miè. Suǒ yǐ bù néng zhě, wèi xīn wèi chéng,

慾未遣也．
Yù wèi qiǎn yě.

[7]

能遣之者，內觀其心，心無其心．外觀其形，
形無其形．
Néng qiǎn zhī zhě, nèi guān qí xīn, xīn wú qí xīn. Wài guān qí xíng, xíng wú qí xíng.

遠觀其物，物無其物．
Yuǎn guān qí wù, wù wú qí wù.

[8]

三者旣悟，惟見於空．觀空亦空，空無所空．
Sān zhě jì wù, wéi jiàn yú kōng. Guān kōng yì kōng,
kōng wú suǒ kōng.

所空旣無，無無亦無，無無旣無，湛然常寂，
Suǒ kōng jì wú, wú wú yì wú, wú wú jì wú, zhàn rán cháng jì,

寂無所寂，慾豈能生，慾旣不生，即是眞靜．
Jì wú suǒ jì, yù qǐ néng shēng, yù jì bù shēng, jí shì zhēn jìng.

[9]

眞常應物，眞常得性，常應常靜，常清靜矣．
Zhēn cháng yīng wù, zhēn cháng dé xìng, cháng yīng cháng jìng,
cháng qīng jìng yǐ.

[10]

如此清靜，漸入眞道，旣入眞道，名為得道，
Rú cǐ qīng jìng, jiàn rù zhēn dào, jì rù zhēn dào, míng wèi dé dào,

雖名得道，實無所得，為化衆生，名為得道，
Suī míng dé dào, shí wú suǒ dé, wèi huà zhòng shēng,
míng wèi dé dào,

能悟之者，可傳聖道．
Néng wù zhī zhě, kě chuán shèng dào.

[11]

太上老君曰，上士無爭，下士好爭，
上德不德，
Tài shàng lǎo jūn yuē, shàng shì wú zhēng, xià shì hǎo zhēng,
shàng dé bù dé,

下德執德，執著之者，不名道德．
Xià dé zhí dé, zhí zhe zhī zhě, bù míng dào dé.

[12]

眾 生 所 以 不 得 真 道 者 ， 為 有 忘 心 ， 既 有 忘 心 ，
Zhòng shēng suǒ yǐ bù dé zhēn dào zhě, wèi yǒu wàng xīn,
jì yǒu wàng xīn,

即 驚 其 神 ， 既 驚 其 神 ， 即 著 萬 物 ．
Jí jīng qí shén, jì jīng qí shén, jí zhe wàn wù.

[13]

既 著 萬 物 ， 即 生 貪 求 ， 既 生 貪 求 ， 即 是 煩 惱 ，
Jì zhe wàn wù, jí shēng tān qiú, jì shēng tān qiú, jí shì fán nǎo,

煩 惱 忘 想 ， 憂 苦 身 心 ， 便 遭 濁 辱 ， 流 浪 生 死 ，
Fán nǎo wàng xiǎng, yōu kǔ shēn xīn, biàn zāo zhuó rǔ,
liú làng shēng sǐ,

常 沈 苦 海 ， 永 失 真 道 ．
Cháng chén kǔ hǎi, yǒng shī zhēn dào.

[14]

真 常 之 道 ， 悟 者 自 得 ， 得 悟 道 者 ， 常 清 靜 矣 ．
Zhēn cháng zhī dào, wù zhě zì dé, dé wù dào zhě,
cháng qīng jìng yǐ.

Daoist Meditation Method of Tranquil Sitting

靜 坐 道 人 法

Master Yinshizi (因是子, 1872–1954)

Tranquil Sitting

靜 坐

Jing Zuo

The following text comes from the writings on the Tranquil Sitting meditation method of Master Yinshizi and is presented in an augmented, edited, and reformatted manner. This new arrangement is a bit more succinct than the original, especially to the beginner, and is in essence an expanded version of the method of meditation prescribed by Yinshizi in his original work published in 1914 in China. It has been included here to provide a clearer view of the deportments of Tranquil Sitting. This method is the very basis of the Daoist meditation method of Sitting and Forgetting (坐忘, Zuo Wang).

Training the Spirit

神 培 訓

Shen Pei Xun

When engaged in meditation, the most essential principle is to concentrate the Spirit of Vitality[31] within the lower abdomen [丹田, Dan Tian]. To achieve successful results with this type of skill is quite difficult because of all the false thoughts we maintain. The beginning of one thought is but the end of another, there not being one moment when these cease.

It is not easy to either alter or subdue the passions. The immediate goal of meditation is to fully subdue these passions; for example, foolish imaginings and false thoughts. When all false thinking is suddenly eradicated, then you will experience a state of thoughtlessness. In what way can this be reached? In every situation you must undertake the task of meditation, exercising tranquility during all mundane matters. Be attentive incessantly.

During meditation, try not to allow desirous or confused thoughts. Put down absolutely everything to fully experience

---

31   *Spirit of Vitality* (精神, Jing Shen) is a term for the refined essences of the Three Treasures (Jing, Qi, and Shen), which in simpler terms is the Qi made capable of moving through the meridians of the body because of its stimulation from Nourishing-Life (Daoist meditation, Qigong, Taijiquan, etc.) practices.

the benefits from concentrating the Spirit of Vitality in the lower abdomen.

In the beginning stages of meditation practice, if false thinking arises, attempt to return to the meditation method. Practice this way repeatedly and consistently. As a matter of course, these false thoughts will naturally diminish over a short time. Eventually, the state of thoughtlessness will be penetrated, which is the foremost vehicle for the attainment of self-realization. However, when you first experience this abstract, contemplative state, don't attach yourself to it. It is only the foundation and not sufficient for complete realization itself, so it is best to treat the experience lightly.

When sitting, close both eyes so that only a fine light can enter and that the tip of the nose can still be gazed upon. This is called "letting the eyes drop." Next, calmly and quietly breathe naturally through the nose until reaching a state in which no sound or sensation of breathing is experienced.

The mouth must be naturally closed. If too much saliva is produced during meditation, carefully divide it into small portions and swallow them separately. Most importantly, keep the mind-intent [attention] on the lower Dan Tian. This will bring great benefit.

As mentioned, take care to lightly close the eyes and then begin counting the breaths. In this manner, one inhalation and one exhalation are counted as one complete breath. Continue counting each breath until reaching ten, then start over at one and count back up to ten, repeating this procedure over and over. This is the manner in which to concentrate the Spirit of Vitality in the Dan Tian, and is called "mutual interdependent mind and breath." Also, this very essential method is called "guarding the mind on the lower elixir." This procedure is an excellent aid for spiritual development.

Continually practice this method and apply the principles for practice. It would do well to memorize them. The result, or goal, as it were, of these subtle techniques is directed at attaining peace and stability of mind, both worldly and spiritually. The techniques herein are neither corrupted nor uncertain. By practicing just this one method, you will be training yourself *terra firma*, and with the necessary moral foundation, enlightened awareness can be reached without hindrance. So, it is best to practice just one method that you find fitting for yourself.

For those who are just beginning in their training of Zuo Wang [Sitting and Forgetting], it is advised, "There is no time in which you do not practice Zuo Wang." Some false thoughts will still come and go even after having practiced sitting meditation for some time.

In truth, an inordinate number of false thoughts will keep returning, some of which you will be totally unaware. You will wonder what are the causes and conditions of them? It can be explained and illustrated in this way. Know that all living beings have false thoughts and that they have them constantly. These false imaginings are comparable to when you encounter some foreign environment, which scatters and confuses your power of concentration. Consequently, you are not too perceptive of things around you. This is precisely what false thoughts do to your concentration. Therefore, when you practice tranquility and are concentrating internally upon the Dan Tian, it is only at this time that you become aware of your false thoughts which suddenly arise and disperse, and even though you may grope at them, you cannot hold on to them.

The following is another type of beginning method for increasing self-awareness of false thinking, but to achieve success you must take the initiative and fully follow the method. Return to contemplating your own mind, thinking, "In what way are false thoughts produced or raised in the mind?" With continual investigation of this question, you will gradually, through a natural course of time and events, acquire the skills of extinguishing a few false thoughts and patterns. There is no need to be apprehensive about this technique, even if you don't fully understand or grasp the purpose of it.

By fully following this method, setting it to work by contemplating the mind in this fashion, and by undergoing long and continuous practice, the way in which false thoughts arise and manifest will clearly be seen. Both naturally and gradually your skills in eradicating false thoughts will improve, even though you may not completely comprehend the causes and conditions of this.

Beginners of meditation experience two kinds of false states and obstacles. The first is confusion, and there is no fixed solution in which to completely settle or eliminate this psychological state. The second is dullness. From time to time you will become drowsy and, for the most part, this state is easy to experience. The only cure for either of these two states is to keep returning and bringing yourself back to the method of meditation [i.e., counting the breaths or investigating the origins of false thoughts]. Otherwise, you will not be able to end these states. Only through constant practice, of either long or short meditation periods, can false thoughts be reduced. Consequently, the easiness of entering states of dullness is a universal obstacle when learning Zuo Wang. It is not at all a rare condition among meditators.

In removing the obstacle of confusion, completely let go of all false thoughts and desires, being utterly empty and sincere when doing so.

How are you to be without false thoughts? By concentrating entirely on one thing, the Dan Tian. Naturally, you will then be able to settle the mind and cure the defect of confusion. For those who hold on to false thoughts and desires, seemingly unable to concentrate wholly on the Dan Tian, it is suggested that they affix their attention to the tip of the nose. This is the proper procedure for stimulating the Spirit of Vitality.

Training the Breath

息 培 訓

Xi Pei Xun

The average person breathes in shortly and shallowly. All the vitality is dissipated within the process of expanding and contracting the upper lungs, thus not allowing full use of the lungs. Because of this, these people are not completely inhaling the air, which in turn does not enable the complete discharge of the carbon dioxide taken into the lungs. This causes the blood to be impure and renders one predisposed to sickness.

The following five sections relate the correct procedures for inhaling and exhaling:

1) When breathing in and out, the breath should be extremely delicate so that even your own ears cannot hear the in and out sounds of the breath.

2) When breathing, don't be hurried to augment the conditions of sinking or slowing down the breath. Just make use of the lower abdomen and let the breath sink and move naturally. Through this you will achieve success. The most important task is to breathe in a natural manner, using no force when doing so.

3) Within the human chest region, between the lower lung area and the upper abdomen, runs the horizontal

membrane of the diaphragm called the "diaphragmatic muscle." Novices often sense a pensive type of breath within the chest. This is a result of the diaphragmatic muscle's lack of exercise. The procedure for exercising this muscle is as follows: When inhaling, breathe through the nose to intake the fresh air. This will stretch and expand the base of the lungs and the lower portion of the diaphragmatic muscle. When exhaling, expel all the foul air by contracting the lower abdomen. This will exercise the upper portions of the diaphragmatic muscle.

4) Within the abdomen are both the large and small intestines. These are extremely soft and pliable and can easily obstruct and hinder the blood circulation. So, by breathing in the air with deep, long, and gradual breaths [deep inhalations and long, gradual exhalations], the air will penetrate into the lower abdomen, making the stomach more elastic. Then the obstructions within the abdomen can be fully corrected and controlled, placing everything in check so that the blood will circulate freely and penetrate into both arms and legs.

5) When breathing, it is necessary to do it through the nostrils, for both inhaling and exhaling. Do not use the mouth. Why? Because the natural tendency of the nose is to breathe, to intake and expel air. In the nostrils are many hairs which filter the mixture of small microbes of dust and dirt, preventing them from entering the lungs during the course of inhaling. Suppose you breathed in with your mouth wide open. First, the beneficial function

of the nose would be wasted. Second, all the small microbes of dust and dirt would easily enter the mouth and into the lungs, causing serious illness and disease. Therefore, it is important to close the mouth not only during meditation, but when performing all ordinary affairs as well.

Stages of Breathing

息 分 期

Xi Fen Li

During meditation the regulation of breath undergoes several stages of processes. Note that all stages make use of the mind-intent leading the breath. First, there is the stage of just counting the breath. This consists of counting each exhalation only. Count to ten exhalations and then start over, doing so repeatedly during the meditation time. If you become confused or distracted, just keep returning to counting from one again until you can count ten exhalations without obstruction during the entire sit. When using this method, constantly sense the breath and counting in the lower abdomen, using the mind-intent to bring the breath into the Dan Tian. In this stage, you can experience one-pointed concentration, and time will seemingly disappear, an hour feeling like just a few minutes or less.

The next stage is to just focus on sensing the inhalation and exhalation in the lower abdomen. Just be aware of each part of the breath, and always return to the method if you become confused or distracted. It is in this stage that you can experience True Breath [真氣, Zhen Qi], wherein the breath seems to work of its own accord, with no physical effort required, and the breath seems incredibly full and active. It will also feel as though only a few breaths were taken during the meditation time. There may also be the sense of not wanting to get up when the sit is done.

The third stage is to sense a small, white cloud or vapor-like substance just below the nose. Imagine that during the inhalation it is dragged in through the nose slightly, and expelled slightly on the exhalation. You must feel that the source of the breath is coming from the Dan Tian, not the nose. In this stage, you can experience a sense of lightness of body and as if time itself is frozen, which initially frightens the practicer.

Fourth stage is entering tranquility, wherein there is only consciousness of the breath, not the physical aspect of breathing. An initial obstacle to entering this stage is the experience of the breath stopping altogether, and one usually panics and grasps onto the breath again. Concentration is then broken. This is very difficult to get past, as it is an inherent attachment to the concept of self and life. When there is no thought of the sit being over or even of when it started, this is entering Zuo Wang [Sitting and Forgetting].

Posturing the Body

身 體 的 姿 势

Shen Ti De Zi Shi

Full-Lotus Posture
(雙 盤 膝, Shuang Pan Xi)

The bones and muscles of young people are soft and pliable enough that it is possible for them to adopt this posture. To complete this posture, put the left foot on the right thigh so that the sole of the foot faces upward. Next, place the right foot on the left thigh. The soles of both feet are now facing upward and the thighs intersect triangularly ["v" shape]. This is called the Full-Lotus Posture for sitting in meditation.

It is essential that the kneecaps are attached directly onto the sitting mat and the body be held naturally upright and erect. Do not sit inclined to the front, back, left, or right.

This type of posture, however, is not easily endured or learned, especially for those of middle age and beyond. For them it is more difficult to perform and they should not force it. Rather, they should gradually train the Full-Lotus Posture by holding the position until it can no longer be endured and then releasing the legs.

Immortal Posture
(仙坐势, Xian Zuo Shi)

When seated, draw in the left heel close to the perineum and set the bottom of the foot to face upward. Position the right leg in front and to the outside of the left leg, with the bottom of the right foot also turned up. Turning the feet will help keep both knees attached to the sitting mat and thus make the posture feel grounded and stable.

Half-Lotus Posture
(單盤膝, Dan Pan Xi)

When seated, place the sole of one foot up on the opposite thigh. Next, place the other foot beneath the other leg to complete the posture. In comparison, this is much easier to perform than the Full-Lotus Posture, but the shortcoming of this Half-Lotus Posture is that it can prevent the kneecap of the raised leg from being able to attach directly onto the sitting mat. After having been seated for a time, the body might begin to lean slightly toward the side. However, it is only necessary for you to be aware of this. Don't feel anxious about correcting this leaning because it is not a severe hindrance.

Cross-legged Posture
(下盤法, Xia Pan Fa)

Suppose an elderly person tried to enjoin the Full-Lotus or Half-Lotus Posture, but could not do them. Perform the Cross-legged Posture instead. Put the two legs crosswise on the underside of the body, as this will do well for them. However, efforts to keep the knees pressed downward onto the mat will most likely come to naught, and it will be easy for the body to become aslant. Always pay attention to this so to avoid and correct it.

Chair-Sitting Posture
(平坐法, Ping Zuo Fa)

If a person's legs cannot be crossed beneath the body, then an ordinary sitting posture on a chair will do. Position both legs so that they hang downward. However, it is important that the feet are on line with one another and equally separated. The bottoms of both feet should be placed flat on the ground. Also, make sure that the thighs are level, with the feet maintaining ninety-degree angles.

This posture is also called, "Collecting the Four Limbs."

Hand Position
(手引法, Shou Yin Fa)

Both hands must be loose and relaxed, without the least bit of tension exerted. Place the back of the left hand lightly over the palm of the right hand, so that both palms are facing upward. Then set the hands on top of the upper thigh area so that the palms appear to be supporting the Dan Tian. [You can also use the Taiji Knot position as shown in the sitting photos, with the right hand grasping the thumb of the left hand.]

Head Position (頭姿勢, Tou Zi Shi)

When practicing meditation, pay attention to the head, neck, face, eyes, and jaws. The head and neck must be held erect and upright, the face should be positioned directly to the front, the eyes closed lightly, the jaws shut so there is no separation between them, and the tongue must be held against the upper palate.

Supine Meditation

思 仰 臥

Si Yang Wo

This is the common position of lying down on the back. In walking, standing, sitting, and lying down, the skill of practicing tranquility of mind is employed in each. It is obviously more difficult to practice tranquility when walking, although it is also not easy to accomplish while standing.

Without attaining one of these six skills of meditative posturing, however, it will be extremely difficult to reach the very abstruse and profound states of tranquility. The active skills of sitting in meditation are the same techniques used in standing, walking, and lying down. Therefore, this procedure should be treated like all the other practices, with the same essential principles being applied.

Practicing meditation in a supine position, even though physically easy, can result in heavy mental dullness. Nonetheless, if there is some inconvenience, or if you are unable to sit in an upright position, a supine posture should be employed as an alternative.

There are two styles of supine meditation: lying on the back and lying on the right side. Lying flat on the back is the common supine position, but it is necessary to remember that the head and shoulders must be properly maintained. Use a high cushion or mat, wear very comfortable clothing, and always maintain self-awareness. The deportments of the eyes, mouth, and so on are all the same as previously described.

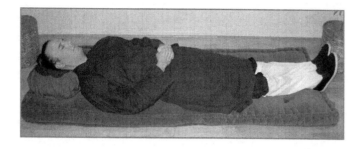

The other method here is to simply lay on your right side. The right or left side can be used. However, after thorough examination it will be discovered that the right side is decidedly best. This is because lying on the left side can produce a continual aching on the left side from the heart being constrained.

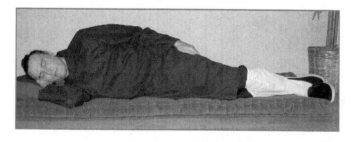

The deportments of the eyes, mouth, nose, and so on are all the same as previously explained. The only difference being that the head and upper body should be bent and bowed forward at the waist. The upper left leg should be less bent then the underside right leg, which is positioned in an arc-like fashion. The left hand should be extended out comfortably along the topside of the left leg. From the knees down, the calves of both legs should be attached loosely, with the right leg stretched out with a slight bend, and the left leg bent further back.

The left hand is extended naturally along the left leg, with the palm facing downward, holding it lightly and loosely by the upper part of the knee. The right hand is held palm up and placed beneath the head like a pillow, but kept loosely attached. It is important to periodically examine your posture and adjust any defects.

Standing Meditation

思 站 立

Si Zhan Li

The deportment for standing is to keep your feet shoulder-width apart. The sides of the feet should be directed straight ahead so that the toes are slightly turned inward. Place the hands in a Taiji Knot and position them in front of the Lower Dan Tian. Keep the head suspended upward, hollow the chest and raise the back, hold the tongue up on the roof the mouth, lower the eyelids, and maintain the breath in the lower abdomen.

Walking Meditation

思 走 步

Si Zou Bu

Walking includes the same deportments as in sitting and standing. Start with both feet together [photo 1]. Then step forward onto the left heel first and inhale [photo 2]. Roll your weight into the left foot as you exhale and raise up the rear right heel [photos 3–5].

[Do this by first turning out the left foot and setting it flat (photo 3), shifting your weight forward (photo 4), then raising the right heel off the ground (photo 5).]

Then bring your right foot forward onto the heel as you inhale [photo 6]. Roll the weight into the right foot and raise the left heel off the ground as you exhale [photos 7–9].

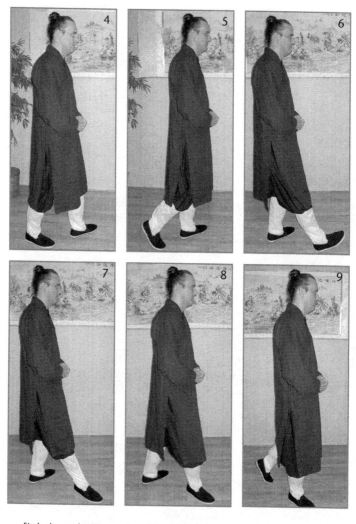

[Inhale and step again with the left foot, repeating walking in this manner for the designated period of walking meditation.]

Rejuvenation Exercises

復 興 行 功

Fu Xing Xing Gong

When a meditation period is over, perform the following Rejuvenation Exercises before leaving the sitting mat.

Rub the hands together vigorously until warm [photo 1] and then cup the hands over the face and circularly rub gently [like washing the face], nine times [photos 2–4]. Then hold the hands over the face and feel the heat penetrating the skin for three breaths [photo 5].

Place the palms on opposite shoulders, then turn and twist the back slowly to each side ten times [photos 6–8].

Stretch out the legs loosely and shake the feet three times [photo 9].

With the back of each hand [held in loose fists], rub the kidney areas vigorously and circularly eighteen times [photo 10].

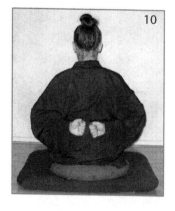

Interlace the fingers and stretch the arms and hands upwards three times [photos 11–12].

Rub vigorously and circularly the sides of both legs, from the hip to the knee, three times [photos 13–14].

Bend the legs and bring up both feet so the bottoms of the feet face each other. Using the thumbs, rub the Bubbling Well Qi centers [the areas in the center of each foot just below the balls of the feet] nine times [photo 15].

Celestial Record

天 文 錄

Tian Wen Lu

The Nine Principles for Attaining the Dao

This text is considered to have been written in the Tang dynasty (618–907 CE) and is attributed to the famous immortal Lu Dongbin (one of the Eight Immortals, depicted above). It is a wonderful, yet short and succinct summary of nine fundamental principles for Daoist cultivation leading to attainment of the Dao.

One: Correcting the Mind

正 心

Zheng Xin

The original nature of a person is the Dao. The mind is but a false intelligence. The mind of a person is dull and apprehensive and so cannot comprehend the Dao or discern where Dao dwells.

First the mind must be regulated, and this simply means to focus and concentrate solely on your method of meditation. From this the Dao will gain a foundation in which to reveal itself, then the Dao can be perfected.

When sitting, focus with full mind-intention. Eventually this focus will also begin to appear in your daily activities, so whether sitting, standing, or walking, simply give those activities all your focused attention.

Two: Curbing Sense Desires

過 慾

E Yu

The Dao is without sense desires. When sense desires arise, turbidity follows. When turbidity and desires cloud the mind, the Dao cannot be clearly perceived. Sense desires result from the longing for life [fear of death], from the longing for self [fear of losing identity and ego], and from the longing for love from others [fear of isolation]. When these longings arise, the Dao becomes independent of the body. Cultivate your mind by curbing these sense desires and contemplate selflessness.

Because of our fear of death, fear of losing our identity and ego, and fear of isolation, we lose the Dao within our selves. When we are selfless, what it is that can die? Who is it we actually lose? When was it you were ever not truly alone? These fears have no true platform on which to stand. They are false and only serve to keep us attached to the life and death of mortality.

Three: Sincerity of Mind-Intent

誠 意

Cheng Yi

The ideal of the Dao is found in sincerity, but the mind-intent must be directed toward the unification of Essence [Jing], Breath [Qi], and Spirit [Shen]. If the mind-intent is not sincere, these three energies will become exhausted.

A person must be capable of making sincere mind-intent a way of life over a long period. When the Dao is part of daily life then the person can gradually enter into perfect realization. The Dao is not difficult, maintaining sincere mind-intent is.

Jing, Qi, and Shen are the Three Treasures. Jing is the physical/sexual energy, Qi is the vital-life breath energy, and Shen is the spirit/consciousness energy. In other words, the Jing is what gives us a body, the Qi animates and warms the body, and the Shen gives us consciousness. The first step in cultivating immortality is the replenishing of these Three Treasures and then uniting them into One.

Four: Settling Anxiety

定 慮

Ding Lu

The Dao must be approached in one way: to first settle all anxiety. When anxieties settle within a person, the Dao has a place to dwell. All other initial measures are just heterodox and only serve to disturb and annoy the highest treasures [Three Treasures], resulting in anxiety remaining unsettled. Because of anxiety, a person is turned upside down and cannot truly cultivate. The attention of the cultivator must be solely on first settling anxiety so to keep to the Dao.

With anxiety we cannot even sit on the mat for the space of a few minutes before turbidity and distractions find their way into our mind. Anxiety is what causes the excuses we make for not having sincerity of mind-intent. It is why we can't curb sense desires, and why we cannot correct our mind. Anxiety is the fear and delusion of loss. Anxiety is the fear and delusion of the mind not being real. Anxiety is the fear and delusion of death and self.

Sense desires then take us away from such fears. Like a con artist, sense desires convince us that only the pleasurable is real and worthwhile.

Five: Fostering the Essence

育 精

Yu Jing

Immortality is in the Dao and immortality dwells within the Essence [Jing] of a person. Why must the Essence be cultivated? Because when Essence is in fullness the Spirit will undergo transformation, the body will then feel light, and the Spirit can roam wherever it pleases.

The Dao of Heaven abides in Yang, the Dao of Earth abides in Yin, the Dao of the Sage abides in immortality, and the Dao of Humanity abides in Essence.

Lao Zi said, "Do nothing to harm the body." Harming the body harms the Essence. Besides blood, saliva, sexual secretions, and tears, Essence also includes the nourishment we give our bodies through food, herbs, fluids, and so on. When we foster our Essence, we are making the body strong and full of youthful energy. Yet, the Essence is normally dissipated through excessive and undisciplined sexual activity, poor nourishment, and excessive toiling of the body. The main source of dissipation, however, occurs through the ears because of the sense-desire for longing to hear beautiful and sensual sounds. Because of this attachment, Daoism teaches to "Turn the Hearing Inwards." When the practitioner of meditation learns to Turn the Hearing Inwards, the Essence will become very strong.

Six: Nourishing the Qi

Yang Qi

The Dao is formless, yet nourishes the Qi. Qi is also formless, yet the Dao produces its abundance. What is formless is of the highest greatness and the most indestructible—the formless is the Dao and it is your Qi. Gather the Qi and longevity can be achieved. With Dao, the Qi gathers. Without it, the Qi disperses. Cultivate the Dao and Qi will follow.

Qi is defined as breath, vital-energy, heat, animation of the body, and vapor. The Qi is like an inherent oxygen within the body that brings a person stamina and vitality. Nourishing the Qi increases the blood circulation. The Qi gives the blood warmth and heat. Through continued nourishment, the Qi will gradually heat the muscles and bones of the body. This heat [Qi] then penetrates into the bones and produces new marrow.

When Essence and Qi enjoin in the body, this fusion produces the Elixir of Immortality, which can then be circulated through the body's Eight Subtle Meridians.[32]

The Qi can also be dissipated and injured through bad breathing habits and from being subject to extreme emotions. The main manner in which Qi dissipates, however, occurs through the mouth from excessive talking, so Daoism teaches us to guard the speech to preserve and nourish the Qi. By focusing on breathing and guarding the speech, the Qi can be made very strong.

---

32   *The Eight Extraordinary* or *Subtle Meridians* (奇 八 脈, Qi Ba Mai) are the meridians stimulated from the cultivation of Internal Alchemy (內 丹, Nei Dan). They were active before the umbilical cord was severed, but dry up, so to speak, after we are born. The Eight Subtle Meridians are not part of the External Elixir (外 丹, Wai Dan) system used in acupuncture, even though some of the meridians and Qi centers use the same names. For a fuller description of these eight meridians, see *Refining the Elixir.*

Seven: Concentrating the Spirit

凝神

Ning Shen

The Spirit abides in the Dao, and the Dao dwells in the Spirit. Concentration will result in being with the Dao; lack of concentration results in dispersion and fragmentation of the Spirit. Cultivate the Spirit by resting in tranquility, then the Spirit will unite with the Qi, and the Qi will unite with the Essence. When all Three Treasures unite, the Dao is realized.

There is a conscious [rational] mind, a mind-intent [will], and a higher consciousness [Heavenly or Spiritual Mind], all three are aspects of the Spirit. The rational mind can either agitate the Spirit [through false thinking] or it can calm the Spirit [through quiet and focused meditation]; the mind-intent can direct the Spirit [through spontaneous natural reactions], and the Heavenly Mind can awaken the Spirit [through cultivation of the Three Treasures].

This Spirit to which Daoism is referring is the Original Spirit, the very essence of one's being when each of us was an infant in our mother's womb. When the umbilical cord is cut, the Original Spirit is cut off as well. Daoist cultivation of meditation is almost entirely about the rediscovery and awakening of the Original Spirit. When this occurs we enter the Dao and attain immortality.

Note that there is no definition of Spirit given here, this is because the Spirit is the Dao within us. The Dao cannot be defined and hence Spirit cannot be defined. The Spirit can only be experienced and perceived in clarity and tranquility because that is where it dwells.

When we were in the womb, we naturally crossed our eyes to look between them to unite the Spirit; we folded the hands over our solar plexus to open it so we could feel our Spirit; and we breathed in our lower abdomen to nourish and stimulate the Spirit. For a few months after coming into this world, we still performed these actions, but soon we were more attracted to external stimuli than internal functions.

We damage our Spirit mainly through the eyes, the means for expressing the Spirit. Wherever our eyes go, so goes our Spirit. In meditation, then, the eyes are directed inwards, which is called "Returning the Light." Returning the Light means to illuminate the Spirit within.

The Spirit is bright when we are infants, but turns murky as the eyes continually express it outwards.

Eight: Contemplating the Void

觀 空

Guan Kong

The teachings of Dao all revert to learning how to contemplate the Void, but what does it mean to contemplate Void? Or even the emptiness of Voidness? Since existence is within a person's mind, it is impossible for mind to communicate with the Dao and all the manifestations of it, so True Void is not really emptiness. As Lao Zi states, "Keep to non-existence, yet hold onto existence." This is the perfection of Dao and contemplation of the True Void.

Regarding meditation, our body sitting at-ease on the meditation cushion represents existence, tranquility. The mind drifting freely from all turbidity, then, represents non-existence, clarity. So it is a matter of keeping to the existence of sitting on the mat, yet equally holding onto a detachment in our minds of the sitting itself.

Do not believe in the false thinking that the Void means you are not sitting on the mat in meditation, nor should you falsely think that your mind should disappear in the Void. Neither of these thoughts are the point of meditation.

The true point of sitting is in realizing that the Dao is experienced when existence and non-existence are "One," not two. When meditating, however, we must keep to existence and hold onto non-existence. This is why it is said, "Contemplating the Void, the Void is not just emptiness."

The *Secret of the Golden Flower* also states, "Emptiness is not empty, it is full of light." Light, then, is clarity and emptiness is tranquility, so keep and hold onto both when sitting in meditation.

Nine: Become the True

Cheng Zhen

If a person is able to cultivate and attain the Dao, he or she will have one hundred years of life. The Dao of Heaven and Earth have their origin in the Great Void. The Great Void is the Dao, and it is neither real nor unreal, and this is true of a person's mind and body as well.

Keep to your cultivation constantly and after a long time there will be an illumination within you like the sun and stars. The Spirit will be able to depart and undergo transformation.

The True is the Dao, and the point of cultivation is to become the Dao. The Dao, though, is neither real nor unreal because it is not two. It is One. Our mind and body are not two either. They are also One [Original Spirit], but it takes continual concentrated sitting in clarity and tranquility to produce the light, the illumination of the spirit.

When the light is produced, the spirit can come and go as it pleases. It is released from the bonds of the false body and mind, and can then transform from mortality to immortality.

For those who sincerely want to enter the Dao and become immortal, they only need to sit. Keep correcting the posture to find the perfection of being completely at-ease, keep the breath soft in the lower abdomen, like a gentle breeze entering and departing from the body, and brush away all disturbances and false thoughts in the mind like a Daoist master using his fly whisk to brush away the flies.

Everyone everywhere can attain these expedient skills from cultivation. The secret of orthodox Daoism lies entirely in these nine fundamental principles.

About the Translator

Stuart Alve Olson, longtime protégé of Master T.T. Liang (1900–2002), is a teacher, translator, and writer on Daoist philosophy, health, and internal arts. Since his early twenties, he has studied and practiced Daoism and Chinese Buddhism.

As of 2015, Stuart has published more than twenty books, many of which now appear in several foreign-language editions.

Biography

On Christmas Day, 1979, Stuart took Triple Refuge with Chan Master Hsuan Hua, receiving the disciple name Kuo Ao. In 1981, he participated in the meditation sessions and sutra lectures given by Dainin Katagiri Roshi at the Minnesota Center for Zen Meditation. In late 1981, he began living with Master Liang, studying Taijiquan, Daoism, Praying Mantis kung fu, and Chinese language under his tutelage.

In the spring of 1982 through 1984, Stuart undertook a two-year Buddhist bowing pilgrimage, "Nine Steps, One Bow." Traveling along state and county roads during the spring, summer, and autumn months, starting from the Minnesota Zen Meditation Center in Minneapolis and ending at the border of Nebraska. During the winter months he stayed at Liang's home and bowed in his garage.

After Stuart's pilgrimage, he returned to Liang's home to continue studying with him. He and Master Liang then started traveling throughout the United States teaching Taijiquan to numerous groups, and continued to do so for nearly a decade.

In 1986, Stuart published his first four books on Taijiquan— *Wind Sweeps Away the Plum Blossoms, Cultivating the Ch'i, T'ai Chi Sword, Sabre & Staff,* and *Imagination Becomes Reality.*

In 1987, Stuart made his first of several trips to China, Taiwan, and Hong Kong. On subsequent trips, he studied massage in Taipei and taught Taijiquan in Taiwan and Hong Kong.

In 1989, he and Master Liang moved to Los Angeles, where Stuart studied Chinese language and continued his Taijiquan studies.

In early 1992, Stuart made his first trip to Indonesia, where he was able to briefly study with the Kung fu and healing master Oei Kung Wei. He also taught Taijiquan there to many large groups.

In 1993, he organized the Institute of Internal Arts in St. Paul, Minnesota, and brought Master Liang back from California to teach there.

In 2005, Stuart was prominently featured in the British Taijiquan documentary *Embracing the Tiger.*

In 2006, he formed Valley Spirit Arts with his longtime student Patrick Gross in Phoenix, Arizona.

In 2010, he began teaching for the Sanctuary of Dao and writing for its blog and newsletter.

In 2012, Stuart received the IMOS Journal Reader's Choice Award for "Best Author on Qigong."

Daoism Books

- *The Immortal: True Accounts of the 250-Year-Old Man, Li Qingyun* by Yang Sen (Valley Spirit Arts, 2014).
- *Daoist Sexual Arts: A Guide for Attaining Health, Youthfulness, Vitality, and Awakening the Spirit* (Valley Spirit Arts, 2015).
- *Being Daoist: The Way of Drifting with the Current (Revised Edition)* (Valley Spirit Arts, 2014).
- *Book of Sun and Moon (I Ching),* volumes I and II (Valley Spirit Arts, 2014).
- *The Jade Emperor's Mind Seal Classic: The Taoist Guide to Health, Longevity, and Immortality* (Inner Traditions, 2003).
- *Tao of No Stress: Three Simple Paths* (Healing Arts Press, 2002).
- *Qigong Teachings of a Taoist Immortal: The Eight Essential Exercises of Master Li Ching-Yun* (Healing Arts Press, 2002).

  Forthcoming
  - *Refining the Elixir: The Daoist Jellyfish Method of Immortality* (Daoist Immortal Three Peaks Zhang Series).
  - *Seen and Unseen: A Daoist Guide for the Meditation Practice of Inner Contemplation.*
  - *Lao Zi's Actions and Retributions Treatise.*
  - *The Supreme One's Yellow Court Scripture: The Internal and External Illumination Teachings.*
  - *The Secret of the Golden Flower.*

Taijiquan Books
Chen Kung Series

- *Tai Ji Qi: Fundamentals of Qigong, Meditation, and Internal Alchemy,* vol. 1 (Valley Spirit Arts, 2013).
- *Tai Ji Jin: Discourses on Intrinsic Energies for Mastery of Self-Defense Skills,* vol. 2 (Valley Spirit Arts, 2013).
- *Tai Ji Tui Shou: Mastering the Eight Styles and Four Skills of Sensing Hands,* vol. 4 (Valley Spirit Arts, 2014).
- *Tai Ji Bing Shu: Discourses on the Taijiquan Weapon Arts of Sword, Saber, and Staff,* vol. 6 (Valley Spirit Arts, 2014).

  Forthcoming Books in Chen Kung Series
  - *Tai Ji Quan: Practice and Applications of the 105-Posture Solo Form,* vol. 3.
  - *Tai Ji San Shou & Da Lu: Mastering the Two-Person Application Skills,* vol. 5.
  - *Tai Ji Wen: The Principles and Theories for Mastering Taijiquan,* vol. 7.

- *Tai Ji Quan Treatise: Attributed to the Song Dynasty Daoist Priest Zhang Sanfeng,* Daoist Immortal Three Peaks Zhang Series (Valley Spirit Arts, 2011).
- *Imagination Becomes Reality: 150-Posture Taijiquan of Master T.T. Liang* (Valley Spirit Arts, 2011).
- *The Wind Sweeps Away the Plum Blossoms: Yang Style Taijiquan Staff and Spear Techniques* (Valley Spirit Arts, 2011).
- *Steal My Art: The Life and Times of Tai Chi Master T.T. Liang* (North Atlantic Books, 2002).
- *T'ai Chi According to the I Ching—Embodying the Principles of the Book of Changes* (Healing Arts Press, 2002).
- *T'ai Chi for Kids: Move with the Animals,* illustrated by Gregory Crawford (Bear Cub Books, 2001).

Kung Fu Books
- *The Eighteen Lohan Skills: Traditional Shaolin Temple Kung Fu Training Methods* (Valley Spirit Arts, 2015).
- *The Complete Guide to Northern Praying Mantis Kung Fu* (Blue Snake Books, 2010).

Downloadable Audio Recordings
(Exclusively through the Valley Spirit Arts website)
- *Setting Up the Foundation* (Instructional Recordings). Includes instructions on the different breathing techniques used for stimulating the Qi for completion of the Lesser Heavenly Circuit. Details on understanding the stages of Three in Front, Three on the Back; 36 and 24 Breaths; and Realizing the Dan Tian are given.
- *Daoist Sexual Arts for Health, Youthfulness, Longevity, and Spirit* (Seminar Recordings). The recordings of these three classes provide useful information on how to apply sexual energy and methods for restoring and revitalizing your quality of life. Health begins with acquiring sexual vitality and accumulating Qi. These audio recordings will give you the necessary tools for accomplishing both. Companion course to the book *Daoist Sexual Arts*. Includes three PDFs of Stuart Olson's translations on the "Rosy Clouds" chapter from *The Immortal*, selected works from *The Plain Girl Classic*, and sections on *Harmonizing the Yin and Yang*.
- *Yellow Court Scripture* (Course Recordings). The information in these 70 audio recordings is simply not attainable anywhere else. Recorded from online classes that Stuart conducted with a student over a year and a half, this commentary on the *Yellow Court Scripture* touches on Daoist philosophy, meditation,

Internal Alchemy, medical Qigong, and the spirit world like no other Daoist material provides.

DVDs

- *Li Qingyun's Eight Brocades* (Valley Spirit Arts, 2014). Companion DVD to the book *The Immortal.*
- *Eight Brocades Seated Qigong Exercises* (Valley Spirit Arts, 2012). Companion DVD to the book *Qigong Teachings of a Taoist Immortal.*
- *Wind & Dew* (Valley Spirit Arts, 2012). This version of Wind & Dew was designed to work in conjunction with the Eight Brocades DVD (also the Li Qingyun version). All three DVDs also work with the teachings in the Setting Up the Foundation Audio Recordings.
- *Taiji Qigong* (Valley Spirit Arts, 2013). Companion DVD to the book *Tai Ji Qi.*
- *Master T.T. Liang's 150-Posture Yang Style T'ai Chi Ch'uan Form* (Valley Spirit Arts, 2014).
- *Master T.T. Liang Taijiquan Demonstrations* (Valley Spirit Arts, 2014).
- *Tai Ji Quan Self-Defense Instructional Program* (3-DVD Set) (Valley Spirit Arts, 2011).
- *Healing Tigress Exercises* (Valley Spirit Arts, 2011).
- *Tiger's Waist: Daoist Qigong Restoration* (Valley Spirit Arts, 2009).

Visit the Shop at Valley Spirit Arts for more information:
www.valleyspiritarts.com/shop/

Also check out Stuart's author page at Amazon:
www.amazon.com/author/stuartalveolson

About the Publisher

Valley Spirit Arts offers books and DVDs on Daoism, Taijiquan, and meditation practices primarily from author Stuart Alve Olson, longtime student of Master T.T. Liang and translator of many Daoist-related works.

Its website provides teachings on meditation and Internal Alchemy, Taijiquan, Qigong, and Kung Fu through workshops, private and group classes, and online courses and consulting.

For more information as well as updates on Stuart Alve Olson's upcoming projects and events, please visit: www.valleyspiritarts.com.

About the Sanctuary of Dao

Established in 2010, the Sanctuary of Dao is a nonprofit organization dedicated to the sharing of Daoist philosophy and practices through online resources, yearly meditation retreats, and community educational programs. The underlying mission of the Sanctuary of Dao is to bring greater health, longevity, and contentment to its members and everyone it serves.

Please visit www.sanctuaryofdao.org for more information about the organization and its programs.

20020745R00092

Made in the USA
Middletown, DE
12 May 2015